THE
REALTORS GUIDE
TO
SHORTSALE
SUCCESS

JEFFREY P. SMITH

The Realtors Guide to Shortsale Success

Copyright © 2010 by Jeffrey Smith

ISBN:1448650860

EAN:9781448650866

First printing, 2010

Printed in the United States of America

ACKNOWLEDGEMENT

I wish to thank my incredible wife Gail for her continued Love and support. Gail encouraged and urged me to share my knowledge of the short sale process so that fewer homes get foreclosed, more buyers get good deals and just as important, Realtors receive the commissions they work hard for by being able to successfully close more shortsales.

I also thank all the Real Estate "Gurus" out there that offer "free" information to hook you in to an expensive seminar or "mentorship" or monthly "University" fees. These people made it possible for me to learn enough to do things on my own without spending a dime of my own money. It only took time to sift through the baloney and hype. Jumping in full time and starting out as a rookie, time was about all I had. They *did* give me a lot of good information for free.

TABLE OF CONTENTS

Foreword

As a Realtor and Mortgage Broker in the state of Florida for 20+ years, I know many Realtors. Whenever I have questions about shortsales or what might happen under different shortsale circumstances, there was always one agent I could depend on to give me accurate answers.
Jeffrey Smith.
I know I wouldn't be selling real estate today if Jeffrey hadn't encouraged me, answered my questions, and taught me how to make pre-foreclosures or shortsales, my specialty.
His experience, knowledge, honesty, and desire to share his "shortsale secrets" has been an inspiration to me and I highly recommend this book to all agents that wants to increase shortsale knowledge, closing ratio for shortsales, increase production, and make better use of your time.

- Mark Galbraith

INTRODUCTION

Maybe you're still in the process of getting your license. Maybe you've been successfully selling residential real estate for the last thirty years. In either case, there has been a real shift in the last 3 years concerning the listing, buying, and selling of real estate. Things are rapidly changing and in some areas, changing on an almost daily basis.

Information is available at the speed of light and the old way of doing things and what worked in the past isn't always what the new informed consumer is looking for. Yes, service will always be king, but the kind of service we provide as Realtors is changing and the consumer is expecting more and different types of service than we previously provided.

The internet is rapidly changing the way we do business. It's very good in some ways, like eliminating the cumbersome printing of huge weekly MLS books and giving us continuously available updated information. In some ways, it is bad by giving out wrong information. Just last week, a homeowner I was counseling concerning the sale of her home told me that she read on the internet that if she did a shortsale on her home that she could go to jail! There are also plenty of "real estate gurus" out there that will have you earning $30-40, 000 per month within 60 days.

The main aim of this book is to help the rookie and realize the benefits of specialization and how to quickly learn the ins and outs of the shortsale process. The book will also to help the seasoned Realtor learn more about the residential shortsale that was very rare until these strange economic times. Every Realtor will benefit from knowing step by step exactly what needs to be done and in what order to bring the distressed property to a happy conclusion for ALL people involved. Learning how to do a shortsale successfully will save you a lot of time and save you a lot of aggravation.

It will also save you a lot of money. A good old saying is, "If you think education is expensive, try ignorance." I promise you that if you follow the guidelines presented here that your closing ratio for shortsales will at *least* double or triple the current national average for successful shortsales. That's book learning. Even learning from *my* experiences will be book learning. *Learning by doing* is the best way, the real way, the true way to learn anything. When you have successfully done 12 shortsales on your own, you probably will no longer need this book as a guide, but may want to refer to it occaissionally.

OVERVIEW

Effective preachers and teachers use a simple formula that seems to work very well when information is being communicated. It is a 3 step process that consists of 1.) Tell them what you're going to tell them, 2.) Tell them, and 3.) Tell them what you told them.

This overview is the information that will be in the body of the book. The summary, (Chapter Ten) will tell you the information that was in the main body, and the rest of the book is the bulk of the information. The importance of goals and how they relate to your entire life will be tied into time management and the importance of systems for efficiency.

The Rookie will be shown not only how to get leads but also how to grade the leads as to the likelihood of turning those leads into dollars. Turning the good leads into listings is relatively simple and time factors will determine *for you* how many listings you can effectively service and how to handle the buyer leads you'll get from these listings. There is always a point at which you can handle *all you can handle* from an individual standpoint. With shortsales, this point comes very quickly.

How to put a shortsale package together, what goes into it, where it goes and why different items need to be in there will be explained as well as the importance of the BPO (Broker Price

Opinion) and why you should never let a BPO person evaluate your listing without input from you.

The similarities of regular homeowners to third party lenders will be seen as the lender can accept, reject, or counter just as a homeowner can and does. In Real estate, as in life, things happen. Veterans know this and the Rookie should be prepared because *nothing ever* goes as smoothly as the big real estate franchises or the real estate gurus proclaim. The good thing is that once you have been through the rigors of a shortsale, a *regular* sale will almost make you laugh at the ease and simplicity in comparison.

If you're anything like me and most book readers, there is a very good chance that the acknowledgement, the Table of Contents, the Foreword, the Introduction and this Overview have all been skipped over to get to the important stuff anyway, so let the real reading begin!

CHAPTER ONE

Goal Setting

Imagine you're at a basketball game and the stands are filled to capacity. The game is about to start, the music and the crowd are at a dull roar, people are talking and trying to find their seat and all are anticipating having a good time. Both teams run out onto the court with excitement but then stop short and look around bewildered. The goals at either end of the court have been removed! The referees tell the angrier by the minute crowd that the NBA has decided that goals aren't necessary and that the teams will be judged on how well they dribble and pass and run.

Ridiculous isn't it? You can't play basketball without goals. Otherwise you're just running, passing, and dribbling. I hope your life isn't like that. If you have no goals you spend all your time running around during the day, passing out at night, and well ... dribbling. How can you be all you can be if you don't know what it is you want to be? When the media interviews someone that has actually achieved anything great, you'll never hear the response like, "Well, I was just was just walking around and suddenly I found myself at the top of Mt. Everest" or, "I was sitting in my rocking chair on the porch and some group of people came over and handed me the Nobel Peace Prize."

No. Nothing great was ever achieved without goals. We were created by God to function best and be our happiest when we are on a journey in life of achieving our goals. Without goals, our lives are joyless and meaningless. Studies show that people that only have the single goal of even just feeding a cat and stroking it till it purrs, live several years longer than those that have no goals at all.

Victor Frankel was a prisoner during World War II and studied the men he was imprisoned with. He later became a Psychiatrist and wrote a book titled' "Mans Search for Meaning in Life." In it, he described how the different prisoners reacted to the stress of incarceration. Under terrible living conditions, many gave up hope and seemingly lost their will to live. They died quickly. Very few survived, (about 1 in 10) and the ones that did survive always had a reason. For some, it was seeing a loved one once more, for some, it was revenge against their captors, and for others it was the belief that if they died, their life would have been lived in vain. Goals are of extreme importance for success at anything. Goals make life more interesting and as in the situation mentioned could mean life or death.

How many goals should you have? One. One for each area of your life. Spiritual, family, business, physical, mental, social. The trick is to make your goals balanced. For example, it's incompatible to decide to work out for one hour each day, read the Bible for an hour each day, spend an hour each day with each of your family members, spend an hour socializing with your friends each day, spend an hour each day in reading that expands your mind or listening to motivational tapes, and then finally devoting an hour each day to your business. First, look at each of these areas and then set a goal on what you would like to accomplish in each area.

To be effective, there are certain things that make a goal more effective and *you* will be more effective in reaching that goal.

1.) The goal must be **specific** – "I want to look better, or I want to sell some real estate this year, or I want to be a better parent" are so general that you and your mind aren't challenged enough to get excited about it. How about, "I shall lose 16 lbs this year, or I shall sell 30 homes my first year in real estate, or I will spend 20 minutes each day really listening to whatever my child wants to say without judging or condemning." Now the goals are specific.

2.) The goals must be **measurable** – This is part of what makes the goal specific. Remember that we stuck a number on the three general things to make them specific. (16 lbs, 30 homes, 20 minutes) The number makes it measurable. If you are halfway through the year, have you lost 8 lbs? Have you sold 15 homes? Have you refrained from making judgments on your Childs' statements and encouraged them to talk to you about their hopes and dreams and anything and everything they are thinking about? (By the way, this is all a psychiatrist does and it is a great relief for the child to know you care) Have you made it up to ten minutes yet? (The Psychiatrist makes it to fifty minutes right off the bat because he's trained and paid do this)

3.) The goals must be **achievable** – You are NOT going to lose 150 lbs in a year if you only weigh 200. You are NOT going to sell 600 homes your first year in real Estate. You are NOT going to be able to give a child 6 hours a day of your undivided attention. (probably not good for them OR you)

4.) The goals must be **realistic** – This takes the goal down from the unattainable to the possible, but still above the probable. If you are 300lbs and should weigh 150, a half hearted diet and exercise program might get you a *probable* weight loss of 16 lbs in a year. If you made the weight loss your number one priority over everything else you could probably lose the entire 150 lbs needed to be lost in one year. A realistic goal (taking into account the weight loss is not THE most important goal to you) would be around 75 lbs for the year.

5.) The goal must be **Timely** – When you set the goal, state a time period in which it WILL be done. Having a goal of losing 5 lbs over the next 5 years is not a real goal. Neither is losing 5 lbs in the next 5 minutes. This is where the prior two components of realistic and achievable come in as the time factor has a direct bearing on how realistic and how achievable the goal is. Let's say you're goal is to sell 1,000 homes. In your lifetime? In the next 10 years? In the next 5 years?

You may have noticed that the 5 components form an easy to remember acronym: SMART.

Specific, **M**easurable, **A**cheivable, **R**ealistic, and **T**imely. Set aside some time right now to think about your goals. What do you want to achieve? How much time will you give yourself to achieve what you want in each of the six areas?

Work on a one month, 12 month, 3 year time frame for each of your goals. Do not practice Wishcraft. What we are doing is not a **wish** list but a **declaration of intention**. State what you intend to accomplish and when. Share your goals with someone who cares if you reach your goals. Share your intentions with your parents, your friends, or someone close to you. If they tell you all the reasons why you can't achieve what you want, never mention your goals to that person again, **just do it!**

Write down your goals and put them where you will see them. Some use the back of business cards or cut business size cards from 3x5's and keep the cards with them at all times. Several times during the day, pull the cards out and go over them. The more you read your goals and keep them fresh in your mind, the better you will do at achieving them.

Regularly review and revise your list. What was once extremely important to you may not be as important to you now. If you have the same exact goals at 20, 40, and 60 years of age, then you haven't changed or grown at all. Write the same goals down in different ways and see how that affects the outcome.

More important than the goals you have written down are the **reasons** why you've written down the goals that you have. For example, if one of your goals is to sell and successfully close 52 homes (one per week average) your rookie year ... WHY do you want to sell 52 homes? Most people would say the money. Okay, why do you want the money? To pay bills? Pay off debt? New car? Vacation? Raise standard of living? All of the above? Keep asking why backward until you have multiple reasons for attaining your goal. For each of your goals, write down all the reasons WHY you *need* to reach your goal. If you only *want* to reach your goal, it's unlikely to happen. By listing all the reasons why the goal is important to you it will become a *need.*

Now think about the persons or resources available that can help you reach your goals. If you are a rookie, I'd recommend starting out your career with one of the franchises that will give you the franchise basic training with no money out of your pocket. This will provide a solid foundation for your career training and give you basic knowledge. You pay for this indirectly as the big franchisors will take a hefty cut from the commissions on your sales. If you don't want to be an actual salesperson but still make some money while you're learning, you can be an order taker. This is otherwise known as a buyers agent.

Now think about the obstacles you are likely to encounter on your way to meet your goal. How will you deal with and overcome them? What will keep you motivated? Do you know the difference between hot water and cold water motivation?

16

Hot water motivation is like listening to a motivational speaker. As the speakers words rain down on us, we "warm" to the idea of getting out there and doing whatever it takes. The longer we listen, the warmer we get and it feels good to think about achieving our goals as we bask in the words. Just like a hot shower though, as soon as the water (words) is turned off, we begin to cool off. Cold reality sets in and the longer the period of time since the hot shower of words, the cooler we are until it becomes a fond memory. This is also known as external motivation since it comes from the outside.

Cold water motivation is almost the opposite. It is cold reality and we don't like to be there. Sometimes we escape cold reality for a time by taking a hot water motivation. This only helps if we then take some kind of action. Taking action is the only way to make progress, overcome obstacles, and reach your goals. Taking action to overcome resistance is what makes us stronger. Internal motivation from within yourself will last and last. Cold motivation doesn't change temperature with cold reality. It accepts what is. The irony is that taking action warms you up and actually doing something positive toward reaching your goal will keep you motivated longer than any motivational speech.

If you've ever lifted weights you know exactly what I mean. Taking action to overcome the obstacle or resistance makes the muscle stronger. It warms you up. As it is in the physical, so it is in everything else. Overcoming resistance or obstacles is what makes us strong as human beings.

The Secret of the Bamboo

Over in Japan, Bamboo is used for many things that we here in America use metal for. Bamboo is very strong, pliable, grows very fast and is lightweight. Bamboo is even used for the scaffolding going up many stories to build high rise buildings. Since Bamboo is so useful Japanese growers wondered if they could make it grow even faster. They decided to create the perfect growing environment. The ground was made optimum for growth, wind barriers were put up because sometimes wind would blow bamboo down. A screen was put over to keep out insects, the exact direction and amount of sunlight coming in was controlled, the amount of watering was exact and they even had a system so that the water would not damage the leaves as rain would often do. Every obstacle to growing was removed. Everything was perfect.

Even the scientists were astounded. The quickly growing Bamboo grew 4 times faster than it normally did! It lgrew so fast that you could literally almost stand and watch it grow! This meant that there would be plenty of Bamboo since Japan could start producing 4 times as much as they had previously. A worker was sent in to chop the Bamboo down so they could begin using it. As he grabbed the stalk to position it for the blade, it crumbled in his hand. He grabbed another and it also crumbled in his hand. One by one every stalk in the experiment crumbled when grasped into little fragments. The experimental Bamboo growing under ideal conditions was worthless! There was never any *resistance or obstacles* for the bamboo to overcome. With no resistance there was no strength to it and with no strength to it, it was worthless.

Perhaps you've known someone that was *given* everything and lived a sheltered life away from the "regular" people. I'm not saying these people grow up to be worthless but if they DO get out in the real world, it's very hard for them to cope. There is little or no strength of character. After you name Ron Howard (Andy Griffith Show) and Ricky Schroeder, (Silver Spoons) can you think of any child star in Hollywood that has grown up to have some semblance of normalcy? *Embrace* the difficulties, they are what will make you strong. Don't whine or pine about how you wish things would work out (*just once!*) the way you want them to and thank God He cares enough about you to send difficulty your way.

Here is a secret of life itself. Things will *never* be exactly the way you want them to be. Things will **never** be exactly the way you want them to be. Things will <u>never</u> be exactly the way you want them to be. Life would be boring otherwise. If *everything* in your life was just the way you wanted it, there would be no reason to *do* anything. Nothing to strive for, nothing to achieve, nothing to hope for. This does not even take into account all the other people in the world that could use your help. How could everything in your life be *exactly* as you want it as long as there are poor, starving, dying, needy people sharing your world? The only people that have absolutely no problems are the ones that are already dead and buried!

Got off on a tangent there didn't I? Let's get back to real estate and I'll tell you something that you'll learn quickly as you start to work with buyers. A true salesman is a listing agent. ANYBODY can be a buyers agent. It takes very little skill, little knowledge, and almost no salesmanship ability. It *will* take a lot of your time and a lot of work and frustration however. It's a matter of having a buyer point to a house and say, "Duh ... I'll take THAT one" and then you write it up. That's an order taker. I've been there. I didn't say, "Did you want fries with that?" but, "did you want the window treatments to stay?" isn't a whole lot different. Let me explain...

When someone is interested in buying a home, they have certain things they REQUIRE and certain things they would LIKE if the price is right and it's available. Take a few minutes and ask the buyer some questions. These are questions they may have thought of casually but never thought of the answers seriously before. "Mr. And Ms. Buyer, what are some of the things that you absolutely must have in a home?" Sometimes you'll have to elaborate like how many bedrooms, baths, lot size, HOA, pool, lakefront, one story, etc. Make a list of the items and then have Mr. And Mrs. Buyer prioritize your list with most important to least important.

Next, ask, "Mr. And Mrs. Buyer, When I find a house that has all your requirements and is in a comfortable price range, what would you like *extra* about the home if it was there? Again, elaborate with things like granite countertops, walk-in closets, extra large lot, pool, extra large kitchen, formal dining room, etc. All the stuff the average person likes, but wouldn't be a deal breaker if that particular thing *wasn't* there. Also have the buyers prioritize this list.

Put both these things together with what area of town (also prioritized by nearness of work, schools relatives, etc. and figure in the cost factor with PITI and the prequalifying letter from a bank or mortgage broker. If you've done this little bit of homework, you should never have to show more than 3-5 homes. I've actually had agents tell me they've shown certain buyers 30, 40, or even 80 houses and haven't found the house they are looking for.

If you ever show more than 7-8 houses to a single buyer, you need to either go over their prioritized list again or talk to them about the realities of their budget and the current market. I did this with one couple I had shown 7 homes to and frankly told them I would show them only one more home. If they didn't want that last home, I would have to quit working with them. I told them politely I *thought* we had built a good rapport and I *thought* I knew exactly what they were looking for, but that it looked like I was missing something... They faced reality and bought the 8th home.

They didn't buy the home because I was a good salesman. No one has ever been talked into, or sold, a home they didn't like. The greatest salesman in the world cannot make someone want to buy a house that they just plain don't like. Let's face it, there are some pretty awful homes out there and some homes would not even be considered except for one thing... price.

The first thing a buyer will ask you when they see a home they like is, "How much is it?" The only thing that will spark interest in a doghouse is if the price is so low it outweighs all the other factors that they just had to have. This is one of the reasons that I truly love shortsales.

In a regular sale, the owner can live in a doghouse and they expect you to sell their doghouse for a castle price because the doghouse *they* call home is so superior to all the neighbors' homes which look just like theirs. You are placed in a situation sometimes where you're showing the home and basically telling the buyers, "I know this isn't exactly what you're looking for but, would you be willing to pay *more* than fair market value for it too?" Of course not, and that is the beauty of shortsales. With a shortsale, you can actually tell the buyers, "I know this isn't exactly what you're looking for, but would you be interested if you could get this house for $20,000 less than similar homes are going for?" ($20k comes out to about $170 per month in payments and that could make or break sometimes concerning living in a particular neighborhood or qualifying for more house than normal.

This can't be done with a regular sale because the owner sets the price and they rarely set the price at or below market. With a shortsale, YOU are the one that sets the price. Isn't that beautiful? The owners don't set the price and the bank doesn't set the price. Personally, after spending years of selling the owners on trying to put a realistic price on their property I almost jumped for joy when I found the price the home was listed at was entirely up to me!

CHAPTER TWO

Time Management, Systems and Numbers

How many times have you heard someone say, "I'll get to it when I get more time, spare time, or free time." Hardly ever happens that the thing gets done right? Why is that? Maybe because there is no such thing as getting *more* time. There are always 60 minutes to an hour, 24 hours to a day and 7 days in a week. There is no such thing as spare time. There is nothing that takes up time without us aging during the process. In other words, we don't go into suspended animation whenever we use "spare" time so it is time taken from our life. The same with free time. No such thing. Time is *never* free because it is *bought* with the *minutes* that make up our lives. There is at least one honest TV show out there which factually states, "This is an hour of your life you'll never get back."

The point I'm making with all this is that we *cannot* manage time. Time will proceed as it always has and we cannot stop it our change it. We can only manage ... **ourselves**. There are several reasons why our lives quite often seem hectic and disorganized. We haven't managed ourselves properly.

The first and foremost reason or cause of mismanaged lives is procrastination. Maybe later, when I get some free time, I'll tell you how to quit procrastinating. Seriously, procrastination occurs when we are faced with doing something we don't like to do, don't want to do, or are afraid to do. The only solution is summed up in the tennis shoe ads, "Just Do It." Once you plunge ahead and get the worst over with as quickly as possible, you will probably begin to enjoy whatever activity it was that you put off. Sometimes the task at hand seems overwhelming. Break the project down into smaller pieces. The answer to, "How do you eat an elephant?" is, "One bite at a time." Take the most distasteful part of what you're doing and do that first. Having the thought lingering in your brain about the unpleasantness ahead will make you less effective on whatever part of the project you are on and will keep you awake at night. Ask yourself why you are avoiding certain tasks and realize YOU are the only one that will make the unpleasant task go away by taking care of it as soon as possible.

My Dad, Phil Smith, was a construction worker and started teaching me the business when I was 12 years old. Bedroom walls and living room walls were such fun and went so fast and we made so much money! We would get into a house or apartment and I would grab all the easy stuff. Then later in the day, it was hot, I was tired and all that was left to do was the kitchen walls, bathrooms and tiny closets. These weren't fun, they didn't go very fast, and I didn't make much money on them. I would want to go home early and start fresh on it the next day. I was miserable after all the "good stuff" was done because only hard stuff awaited me. My Dad on the other hand, always started with the worst stuff first. He told me he did that so he would have the "good stuff" to look forward to when he was more tired in the afternoons. The "bad stuff" is done as quickly as possible to get to the good. If the "good stuff" is done first, the "bad stuff" seems to take forever. He learned this habit from HIS Dad who had grown up on a farm and, as you could suppose, had "good chores" and "bad chores." By the way, my grandfather, Albert Smith, was one of the few people to ever receive the Congressional Medal of Honor while he was still alive.

For those of you that may have a bad habit you want to get rid of, there is a great little book out called, "Just Stop It!" Keeping these 6 words in your mind at all times will change your life. For the things you need to get done, "Just do It!" For any bad habits you need to stop, "Just Stop It!"

The second thing that happens to all of us are interruptions. We can be doing research on the web looking for something in the MLS and something distracts you. Maybe a phone call, maybe an e-mail message. You turn your attention to the distraction, and wham, the distraction has you thinking in a totally different direction because whatever distracted you needs your immediate attention. You take care of that little business and your mind has a thought that pops up triggered by the previous distraction. Here's the kicker ... *not including* the time you spent *on* the distraction, it takes the average person ten minutes to get back to the same level of focus and concentration they had prior to the original distraction. This is one of the reasons why some people have trouble working at an office and it's also why some people have trouble working out of their home. With the virtual office that is available today, many people like myself work almost totally out of the home(the kids are grown) and only go into the office maybe once a month for the clients that want to meet me there. Turn off your e-mail notifier and only check it at selected intervals.

One way to keep phone interruptions at a minimum is to make your return calls all at once. I turn my phone off and only turn it on every 2 1/2 hours for however long it takes to return my calls and take any calls that come in while I'm doing this. With a pad nearby, I write down all the messages, prioritize them and then return the calls. This is the same pad that I keep one of my most important tools for managing myself, the to-do list. Back when business people were beginning to develop ways to become more efficient, a system was developed that is very simple, but very effective concerning task accomplishment and staying focused. It is still in use today. This is how it is done:

Write down everything you need to do tomorrow. Now out of this entire list, pick out the six things that are most important.

Number by order of importance each thing you need to do. The most important thing is number one, the next most important thing is number two and so on.

When tomorrow comes (and it will or you can sue me) start with the 1st item and work on that item until it's completed. When that item is completed, start on number two and work on that item until it is completed and so on.

There are exceptions of course just like in everything. For example, if you need to talk to a loss mitigator and you're in Georgia and they are in California, don't twiddle your thumbs waiting for them to arrive at their desk at 8 a.m. California time while it's noon where you are! Another time saver is when you have say 3 or 4 deals with a particular lender, go ahead and knock them all out with one phone call instead of calling lender A and then lender B and then back to lender A again, even if that is the order of importance. Group the projects together on your priority list, and get on and off the phone without the extra chit-chat. Set aside time to look at letters, e-mails and other paperwork-type stuff and deal with it *one* time. Delete or save right then and there. You just don't have time to go back later and look at something that *may* be kind of interesting. It's either important or interesting enough to save or it's not. Remember that "free" e-course you signed up for? They sold your e-mail address to others. Yes, they hate spam as much as you do but it isn't spam when it's a different company affiliated with them that contacts you to buy stuff you don't need. See if you can get a blocker because marked as spam doesn't do much of anything.

Focus on the important things, your goals, and don't worry so much about what seems urgent. If you keep reacting to everything, you start running around putting out one "fire" after another. Keep your goals in mind and keep heading toward the achievement of them by being proactive and initiating the progress yourself. The world will turn without you or me. So often other agents do what I used to do. React to everything as if it were an emergency. You have an evening planned for a nice dinner and a quiet evening with your spouse. Someone calls up and says come list my house tonight or I want to see the listing that you have on Blank street tonight and boop! You're gone and your spouse feels like something else is more important to you than them. Friend, *nothing* is more important than the people you love and letting them know you love them by actions.

Specializing – a Niche For You

One of the fastest ways to achieve your goals is to specialize, develop a niche. Developing a niche is a matter of learning all you can about your niche, focusing on your niche, practicing your niche almost exclusively. A cardiologist, an ear, nose, and throat doctor, a brain surgeon, are all specialists. They all have vast knowledge far beyond what other doctors have *in their specialty*. They all practice almost exclusively within their specialty and they all make a whole lot more money than a general practitioner.

As a professional yourself in the Real Estate field, you can be a general practitioner and do a little bit here and a little bit over there and not make much money. You can also specialize and make a whole lot more than the general practitioner. If you're reading this book you may be considering the niche of shortsales.

That's great because after these first two chapters which will show anyone how to be generally successful at just about anything, the rest of the book will deal almost exclusively with the shortsale process. I will not cover Commercial real estate, industrial, vacant land, auctions, leasing and rentals, businesses, personal buying or selling, exchanges, or some referral system.

This book will cover residential shortsales only and I'm going to narrow the residential field down considerably from what is available so that you can focus on the type of property that changes hands most frequently . Trust me, there will be much more business than you can handle even after I show you the extra rewards in specializing within the specialty of shortsales. By focusing on this specialty within the specialty, you won't waste a lot of time and be spinning your wheels as you learn some new aspect of real estate that just doesn't happen that often and is already covered by other agents that DO specialize in the areas you're going to ignore.

If your MLS gives the statistics on properties sold, you will find that the majority of property is of a certain type and a certain price range. This is where you'll concentrate. Yes, selling a shopping mall may result in a million dollar commission but you and your family will starve to death waiting for that to happen. Just as a car salesman would rather make a regular commission selling a car regularly, if they went into selling airplanes, the commissions would be much higher but may or may not be there. The bigger the price tag, the more infrequent the sale.

With the exception of a friend, referral or relative begging me to list their home and sell it for them I do *not* list or sell:

Mobile or manufactured homes

Homes on more than 5 acres

Condominiums

Townhomes

Frame houses more than 25 years old

Homes smaller than 900 square feet

Homes more than $400,000 in current market value

Homes less than $50,000 in current market value

Homes that have bedrooms that one must walk through to get to another portion of the house.

Vacant lots or land

Multiple units (2-3-4 or more units)

Of course, you may want to tack any of these on to the single family houses I'm suggesting you concentrate on, but for the most part, I've found them to be time wasters. You have a learning curve for each one and you tend to *lose your focus* with distractions. There are fewer buyers for these properties and several of the categories have agents that specialize in them already. Short sales *can* be done on any of them but like the guy that said he robbed banks because that's where the money is, I concentrate on the *other, regular* houses for the same reason.

Numbers

Some of the greatest salesman that have ever lived agree, sales is just a numbers game. Just as I mentioned above about choosing to specialize in the homes that had the greatest proportion of buyers is a smart thing to do it's important to know what numbers you're dealing with.

It will be important to answer these questions:

What is the average sales price of the homes selling in your area? How many homes are for sale in your area? How many homes sell each month in that area? What is the average commission paid out per side? How much of your commission is left after your broker takes his cut? How much money do you want to make in the coming year? After taxes and expenses? How many closed sides will you need to achieve this goal? What is the fall through rate? Double it, if you're a rookie. *Now* how many closed sides do you need after taxes and expenses? How much time is spent on a regular listing from the day of the listing until closing? How much time is spent on a shortsale from the time of the listing until closing? How many leads come in from sign calls? From the Internet? From open houses? From floor duty? How many listings can you handle at any given time? How many buyers? How much extra should you earn when hiring an assistant for 10-20 hours per week? What part of your work can be delegated to an unlicensed assistant? What part can be delegated to a child of yours that will do it for the sheer joy of working with you? (;-)

Answering the above questions will set you well on your way to knowing just what you will need to do to achieve your goals. Many of the answers will be specific to your area but I can give you some of the answers right now.

In a normal market, a regular listing that comes under contract from a qualified buyer has a fall through rate of about 18 percent or an 82% success rate. This does not take into account that only about half of regular listings even come under contract the first time they are listed. Only about 60 per cent come under contract the second time they are listed. A regular listing takes about ten hours of work from the day the listing is signed till the day of closing.

A shortsale listing should have at least one purchase offer on it. It is normally listed only one time. The fallout rate for shortsales is very dismal nationally. It is 77%, which means it has a success rate of only 23%. In addition, the average shortsale takes about 40 hours from the time it's listed till the day of closing.

I personally have the same closing ratio with shortsales as the national average on regular sales. Reading this book and implementing the suggestions should enable you to double or triple your closing ratio over the national shortsale average. I believe the dismal national average of shortsale success is due to the fact that many agents simply do not want to do them because they are 4 times as much work and due to the agents lack of specialized knowledge they close about ¼ as often as a regular sale.

In my state of Florida, more than 50% of all the single family residential sales are currently either a shortsale or a bank owned property. That leaves very few homes that are "regular" listings. It is also very tough for the average homeowner to compete in a market like this because they simply cannot afford to drop the price of their home to market level. Not to mention that the market level keeps dropping due to the influx of shortsales and bank owned homes!

Agents ask me all the time how I can stand to work shortsales exclusively and the answer is simple. When I moved to this area it was just as the market crashed and even though I could get listings, homeowners refused to wake up to the fact that the value of their home was dropping rapidly. As a result the only regular listings that were selling were selling to buyers that were also not aware that prices had dropped rapidly. So I had a choice. Specialize, do a lot of work and make some good money, or do little work and make little money as a general practitioner. To me, it was a no brainer but many regular agents refused to accept the fact that the market had changed drastically and that the old way of doing things was simply not going to make it. Many of the

Realtors that had been in the business for years hung on by the skin of their teeth by the referral business they had built up.

By the way, the first year that I decided to work Shortsales exclusively, I made a nice income and never once worked with a buyer. All my sales were from the listing side and this made it much easier to organize my time. The sellers I worked with would see me on my schedule and a simple phone call once a week would keep them updated. With buyers, they always want to look at houses on *their* time and if you don't answer stupid questions about the cute house they just drove by that isn't suited for them or you would have included it in the list of homes for them to look at, they **will** find an agent that will say, "how high" every time they say, "Jump!"

In any given regular year, the average Realtor board will lose about 33% of its members and about 40% will join for the first time for a net gain of about 7% membership. Last year, 2008, the average Realtor board in Florida had a net loss in membership of about 23%. Part of this loss was directly due to the fact that many refused to take on the burden of educating themselves about shortsales.

It only cost time to learn. Why? There are plenty of "real estate gurus" out there that promote themselves, their seminars, their mentorship. The way they convince prospects to sign up for these expensive deals is to convince the prospects that they "the guru" have a wealth of knowledge that will make the prospect an overnight success. The good thing is that they offer up some free information for you to listen to their pitch and see what it is they want you to buy into.

There are many different gurus out there on the internet and it would be stupid if they all offered up the same free information. By offering *different* information, the gurus make it seem like they have something the other gurus don't have. By getting all the free information from the many different come ons, the average person can find out all the information they need to know for a successful shortsale. I'm putting it all in this book anyway so you don't have to spend the hours I did sifting through all the baloney and come ons to get to the real meat of how to do it. I'll reveal one of the biggest secrets to you right now but I must ask that you KEEP it a secret:

There

are

no

secrets...

A secret is something that nobody else knows. Many people know how to do a shortsale successfully and the information is *not* secret and is available for free. Buying this book just saved you all the time of searching and researching. All the gurus promise secrets and stuff "never before revealed" but thanks to the internet, there isn't any system or idea that someone is doing that someone else hasn't put on you tube or a cheap or free e-book. When people find out that they have been tricked into spending a ton of money to "learn the secrets", and then find out the truth, some of them turn right around and give that "gurus secrets" away for free as payback. You'll find that if you google the gurus name and scroll down past his own advertisements, you'll find what some of his students have to say about him and this will help you decide how much of what he says you're going to "buy" into.

Chapter Three

Turning Leads into Listings

There are many sources of leads for the shortsale listing and just as you can pick up leads for a regular listing, these same sources are available to you as a shortsale agent and more! There are slightly different approaches according to the state you're practicing real estate in. The first thing you should do is find out if you are in a *judicial* or *non-judicial* foreclosure state. There are two main differences between these.

In a judicial foreclosure state like Florida and New York, the foreclosure process takes much longer because everything must be done properly and legally and goes before a judge with an actual hearing and being served official lawsuit papers. In Florida, it can take between 8 months to a year or more before foreclosure takes place. In New York, at least one year is normal. On the other hand, Texas is non-judicial and the property can typically go to foreclosure as soon as 21 days after the notice of default is served.

The time frame is a big difference and a lot of people are glad they live in a judicial state. On the other hand, many people are glad they live in a non-judicial state for a different reason. In the judicial state, if a property actually goes through foreclosure, the lender always files a deficiency judgement against the borrower. The lender is then allowed to pursue the borrower with all legal means to collect the difference between what was owed on the property and what the property ultimately sold for after foreclosure. A judgement is good for ten years in Florida and can be renewed for another ten years. In the non-judicial state if it actually goes to foreclosure, the lender is done and has no further recourse to collect anything on the difference. Usually when a shortsale occurs, the lender will simply mark in the credit report something along the lines of, "Account settled. Not for full amount" This is an excellent reason for the homeowner to do a shortsale since the deficiency judgement is rarely filed. In a foreclosure, it is *always* filed.

Occasionally, the lender will state in the approval of sale letter that the homeowner understands that they (the lender) is reserving the right to pursue the borrower for the difference. This worries the homeowner needlessly. The lender knows the homeowner has no money to spare at this time so hopes the borrower will win the lottery or something in the next year or two. Without a judgment filed, the lender (I've been told by an attorney) loses his right to pursue after 2 years and reserving the right to pursue is mainly to appease the stockholders the lender has to answer to.

The For Sale By Owner

The first lead source of leads for *all* realtors is the For Sale By Owner or FSBO or fizzbo as it's pronounced. The only thing good I can say about For sale by owners is that most of them are serious about wanting to sell their home. Take a different approach than the other realtors. Find out first if the owner is in default. If they are, find out how much the owner is asking and how much he owes and what the home is approximately worth.

Sometimes the home is worth more than they owe but the owner is still asking too much or doesn't know what they are doing to get a sale. Usually, they are selling on their own because the home is worth $106,000 and they owe $100,000. They hope they will be able to walk away with 6k because of the difference. It just doesn't work that way.

1.) Only a totally uninformed buyer would make a full price offer to a for sale by owner.

2.) The owner isn't taking into account the constantly rising closing costs which are currently about 3% of the sales price. (and that's just on the selling side)

3.) The owner isn't taking into account any repair costs which a professional inspection may incur.

4.) The owner isn't taking into account any back payments, late fees, or attorneys costs if they are behind at all.

5.) The owner rarely takes into account that his home is NOT worth more than the identical home in the same sub-division which sold for $105,000 last week.

6.) Homeowners traditionally ask 6% more than their home is worth and then tell prospective buyers that if it doesn't sell soon, they will put it with a Realtor and then the price will be 6% even more.

Think of the logic of that last one. A home is worth $106k. The owner thinks because it's HIS house its worth $110k. He knows the average buyer will offer about 5-10% less so he jacks the price up to $118k. Now he tells the prospective buyer that if it doesn't sell, he'll put it with a Realtor at $125K. Meanwhile, there is a short sale and an REO (Real Estate Owned, bank owned, already foreclosed) property just down the street with the same floor plan in the same neighborhood for $99k!

The FSBO is dreaming and wishing and hoping. Unless the market is rapidly appreciating (2-4% per month) which it is not now happening nor will it in the foreseeable future. This homeowner needs to be educated about the realities. In fact, in my area of Lake County, Florida, homes have been DEPRECIATING 2-4% per **month** since October of 2007. Many homes are worth about half what they were worth in 2006. Using the old square footage average, at the height of the market, homes sold for about $160 per square foot. (including lot) Now they are currently selling for about $75 per square foot or less (including lot) Of course, this doesn't take into account swimming pools, exclusive neighborhoods or acreage.

In any case, if a seller is asking at, near, or below what is owed on the property (including back payments if behind) that seller is a prime candidate for a shortsale. The owner is not going to net out anything on the shortsale of their house anyway and almost all lenders require a home be listed with a MLS participating Realtor to qualify for the shortsale.

To find out how much is owed on the property and if the owner has received an L.P. (lis pendens)or N.O.D.(Notice Of Default) you must go to the court records. If you are in a progressive county all the county court records should be freely available online. If not you may have to pay a small fee for online access or actually, physically, go down to the courthouse. (ouchski)

L.P. **L**is **P**endens is Latin and roughly means lawsuit pending and NOD **N**otice **o**f **d**efault means just that. The homeowner is in *default* of the mortgage loan agreement and the lender is pursuing their rights concerning the house. The house being the security instrument for the loan. FSBO's will make up a very small percentage of your shortsale listings.

The Expired Listing

Prior to getting into shortsales, the expired listings were my favorite and main source of income. First of all, you already know that they are serious about selling their home. Second, you know they are already somewhat educated on the value of using a

Realtor. Expireds can be a good source of regular listings and some of these can be converted to shortsale listings.

If a home has been on the MLS and in the internet data bases for any length of time and the listing expires, there is one reason and that is, PRICE. No matter how fantastic a house is or how terrible it is, It still boils down to what a ready, willing, and able buyer is willing to pay for the house. Even I have caught myself thinking, "this dump will never sell" but I should have added, "at this price." ANY dump will sell at the right price. The challenging opportunity is to convince the owner that the dump they are trying to sell is not a castle.

When calling on expireds, I won't take one that doesn't fit the parameters of my shortsale requirements mentioned earlier. This eliminates a few. Next, if the property is owned outright (doesn't have a mortgage) or the mortgage is 60% or less of rough guesstimate current market value, I'll pass if the owner is adamant about the price. Unless they are in default, no matter what size the mortgage is, get to these owners as quickly as possible

Let me just interject something here that I learned first hand from Zig Ziglar. (I worked with him directly and for some of you young whippersnappers, he was considered to be one of the greatest salesman of all time)...When is an appointment an appointment? In other words, suppose you call someone up on a Monday night and set the time to talk for Wednesday night, 2 days later. Now, suppose you are at someone's door on Monday night and they invite you in to talk to them about selling their house. Is there any difference between an appointment that is for 2 days later and one that is for 2 seconds later? Personally, I think the one for 2 seconds later is far better. When I'm at the door and they invite me in to talk, I know I've got the listing. What do these homeowners say after they've signed the listing agreement? They say, "I've gotten plenty of calls and letters from people saying they wanted to "help" me but you are the only one that came to see me and you're here right now."

When you are at the homeowners door, (or anytime else for that matter) be careful to be 100% honest with them and to not say **anything** derogatory about any other agent. Once you have been in the business for awhile, you will find snakes in the grass. There will be other Realtors that you simply would prefer to not do business with, but this is not the homeowners business. Say nothing, or say something nice like, "oh sure, I know so and so, he/she is a hard worker." You didn't say he/she was a good Realtor or an honest Realtor.

I know a lot of Realtors disagree with the in-person going to the door and knocking approach. I am *not* advocating knocking on doors randomly or even going door to door in a "farm" area. The doors you will be going to will either be a FSBO, an expired listing, or someone that has received either a notice of default or a lis pendens. The FSBO wants to sell, the expired wants to sell, the NOD homeowner *probably* needs to sell. I said *probably* because most homeowners aren't aware of the many options available to them. In most cases, the shortsale will be their best option but there are some that a short refinance (loan balance reduction) or a bankruptcy would be better for them in the long run. A loan modification is usually only good if the value of the house hasn't dropped tremendously below what is owed on the property.

A lot of Realtors like to work the expireds daily. This is a good idea if you work expireds because the competition is fierce. Some Realtors will tell the homeowner just what they think the homeowner wants to hear, list the home at any price and then spend the entire listed time trying to get the owner down to a reasonable market price. Waiting one day or two and you'll find the property has already been re-listed by the early bird. I have more pre-foreclosure leads than I can handle so I haven't talked to a FSBO or expired listing in almost 2 years. (unless they were in default)

Because the court records are put on the internet daily for my county, I like to get my daily leads for LP's and try to see them as quickly as possible. When checking the online records, there is no way I could see all the LP's that show up on a daily basis even with the elimination of properties I no longer work. (mentioned earlier) If you work in an area that has far fewer foreclosures, you may want to expand your acceptable properties or include regular FSBO's and expireds.

I'll give you the numbers that I've personally experienced so you'll have some idea of what to expect. It's possible you'll do better or worse but these are the numbers I'm currently experiencing.

About 25% of all the homes you go out to visit will already be vacant. If you want, you can waste your time trying to track these people down. The exception is if there is a for sale or a for rent sign out front. The people with the sign out front are ready for a short sale. *If* you can locate them, try to find some that are cooperative. Most are not. They think if the bank can't find them then the foreclosure won't happen or follow them.

About 8-10% of people that are living in the home that is headed for foreclosure are renters. This, unfortunately, has also turned out to be a dead end. If the renters continue to pay, they make it difficult to show the home because the sooner it sells, the sooner they have to leave. If the renters aren't paying rent, they have no reason to leave or let you show the house.

Normally, the process server that gives the tenants the NOD or LP tells them that they should stop paying rent to the homeowner. Once the renters hear this, it's unlikely that the homeowner will be able to pull out of foreclosure with no rent money coming in and no way to legally evict. In some ways, you can't blame the tenants to save their money for first, last, and security at the next place, not to mention the cost of moving. If the tenants themselves are interested and qualified, you *may* be able to write up an offer with them as the potential purchasers. You still need the current owners permission and cooperation in doing a shortsale.

Send out letters or flyers to people that have received the NOD or LP. Offer a free consultation concerning Loan balance reduction, loan modification or shortsale.Each letter including postage runs about 55 cents in cost. Mailing out 50 letters at a cost of less than $30 has always gotten me 1 listing on average. I prefer spending $30 bux upfront compared to giving away 25% of the total listing side commission in the way of a referral.

Remember what I said about being selective? This is another example. I send one kind of letter out to homeowners that have the tax bill sent to the home in pre-foreclosure. I send a different kind of letter to a homeowner with a different tax address than the property being foreclosed. If the tax address and the pre-foreclosure property are different addresses, I do not drive to either address but let the letter do the talking. When you actually talk to a homeowner at the door, one out of four should end up giving you the listing. You will also experience the "sweet one" if you keep at it long enough. By that, I mean, you pull the name and address off the court records, go to the door, and the homeowner greets you and invites you in. 98% of the time, you should get the listing on the spot if they invite you in to talk.

Included in another appendix is the script I use when at the door to reassure the homeowner that I'm not there to harass them, ask them to give me their house, or ask for any money. I am simply there to tell them that they can stay longer than they think without paying and that there is a no cost way to avoid foreclosure and the inevitable deficiency judgment. If they don't invite me in or say the usual, "we're working it out with the lender" you then smile and say, "I can appreciate that and I really hope that things work out for you. If things *don't* work out for you or if you just want to ask any questions, let me leave my brochure and refrigerator magnet card with you so you'll have my number, okay?"

I have a simple brochure giving the options available to the homeowner that prints up on my own printer/copier with slightly heavier than regular paper in pastel colors. I also use a magnet attached to the back of my card because I can't tell you the number of times I've been to a house and the people say they know a Realtor but the card was shoved in a drawer somewhere and they just can't find it. I don't use calendar magnets because after the year is up the calendar gets tossed along with your name. I also use pens from National Pen co. with my name and a message of pre-foreclosure at no cost and my phone number. A nice pen runs about 45 cents but I would wait to order them till after your first closing if you're strapped for cash. The magnets are cheap (I think it was 60 bux for 2,000) and it'll be a long time before you need magnets again. See if any co-workers would like to split the cost 2 or three ways to cut your cost down. Brochures are about 5 cents apiece that you can make as you need them.

These statistics were from the NAR. The average listing agent spends about 10 hours of time and 23 phone calls for every *regular* listing that sells. The average shortsale listing takes 44 hours and 77 phone calls till closing. The information I give you in this book should cut that time in half. (based on the average time I spend)With a national closing average of 2 out of 10, it's easy to see why the average agent just doesn't want to do shortsales. Part of the dismal record for shortsales is the fact that many agents have no good information on how to actually do the shortsale and the failure rate makes other Realtors scared to bring a buyer to a shortsale property because **they don't know** what the listing agent doesn't know.

When taking the listing, it's important to add some verbiage which will save you a lot of time and trouble. First of all, I make it a point to tell the homeowner that there is a zero cost for withdrawal at any time. Situations change and if the lender talks them into a loan mod or an attorney talks them into bankruptcy or they win the lottery, you aren't there to stop them from what they believe is best for them. At all times, you are there to help them the best you can.

Second, I add in a clause that says the owner approves of any and all price changes as needed to sell the house. (No need to get a signature again for each price change) This is a very stressful time for the homeowner and your reassuring and confident manner will go a long way to calm and soothe them to know they have put themselves in the hands of a professional that cares about them and their situation.

Third, I add a clause that says the seller agrees to sign any purchase offer approved by the lender. In my part of the country, if the seller *signs* the purchase offer the listing must be pended and that almost always prevents further offers coming in on the property. If there are no other offers on the property your situation is tenuous. Buyers sometimes panic and bolt. Buyers sometimes can go no higher on the price offered and the bank counters for considerably more. Buyers sometimes don't qualify for the loan. Buyers sometimes die. (One of my buyers did) Buyers sometimes make a good offer but by the time the lender approves it, the market has dropped and now the property isn't worth what the buyers originally offered.

So things happen. The importance of getting backups happened to me about 6 months ago when the buyer that was actually in 4th position actually ended up being the one to complete the purchase! If the seller doesn't sign the offer, it remains an offer. If the seller signs the *offer*, it becomes a *contract* and the listing must be pended.

Sometimes the lender requires the seller signature before they will review the shortsale file any further. Usually though, I have found that the lender only asks for the seller signature just prior to verbal approval. Once, the lender didn't have the seller sign the purchase contract until the actual closing. This was a cash deal though so an exception. Normally, the new buyers' lender requires a completely executed contract before they will proceed with the loan process.

The day you take the listing, go ahead and get the Authorization signed by the seller. The sellers' lender won't talk to you or discuss the loan or the property without written authorization. (see appendix) The day you take the listing give the client a list of all the paperwork you'll need from them concerning the paperwork. Leave a sample hardship letter because most of them will tell you they have no idea what they need to write. I'll go over everything needed for a proper shortsale package in the next chapter.

When you take the listing, quite often the seller will tell you, "oh, I'm leaving the range, dishwasher, refrigerator, microwave, ceiling fans, etc." smile politely, say, "that's fine" and then under *appliances included* put NONE. It will save you a lot of grief and aggravation. I bought a few refrigerators and a couple of stoves before I learned that lesson when I first started doing shortsales.

In a regular sale, the owner has to pony up the appliances or acceptable cash if they have agreed to leave them and they are part of the sale. Big legal consequences if they don't, and or money withheld at closing. (if it closes) If it doesn't close for the sole reason that the seller wouldn't pony up for appliances they agreed upon in the sales contract, the seller is still liable to you for

51

the commission. In a shortsale, the lender is paying the commission to you and the seller isn't receiving any money that can be taken away so guess who normally ends up footing the bill when it was *your* seller that took the appliances out and sold them 2 weeks before closing saying, "Golly, I thought they were mine to do with what I wanted. You never told me I had to leave the appliances." Anyway, it comes from your commission so when an offer comes in and asks for all the appliances, you must get it removed from the contract. Point out that the listing says no appliances included but the seller **may** leave some behind, you just can't guarantee it.

Just as property condition is reflected in the purchase offer, so can the loss of appliances. FHA *does* require a stove if they are going to put a loan on the property. When I've had to buy appliances, I don't buy top of the line or even middle of the line. I buy anything that looks good, works, and fits no matter what was there previously. Buyers also try to sneak in washer and dryers also even though they are not mentioned in the listing either.

When you list the home, this is absolutely the best time to get a key, put it on lockbox, and/or make arrangements for the house to be shown on a moments notice. Men are sure different than women when it comes to letting the house be shown. The woman always wants to straighten up the house before anybody sees it. The man just wants to make sure his sports game on T.V. is not going to be interrupted. I say a moments notice because you'll find that *some* Realtors will drive buyers all over the place and let them point and say, "I'd like to see *that* one" without any idea how much it is, how many bedrooms and baths, etc. and then the agent calls you (because your number is on the sign) and they don't have MLS access in their car (because they haven't tech'd up yet) so could they please see the house? The buyers are always "only in town for one day" and they have suckered some agent into being a tour guide and they really have no intention of buying anytime soon. I'm not cynical against buyers or agents. It's just a fact that many new, part-time, or inexperienced agents will do almost anything for the carrot of a commission dangled in front of them.

Now that you have the listing, what are you going to price it at? There are two schools of thought on this. The first is to put the home on the market with a list price about 10% under market. Next, put in an investor or dummy offer to "get the ball rolling" and have the lender start working your shortsale. Next, wait and see if the lender is willing to accept this lowball offer or, if not, what they will counter at. Meanwhile, while all this is going on, hope that you get a legitimate offer on the property that is somewhere near or even above what the bank says they'll take. I no longer use this method because all too often it would backfire. If no legitimate buyer showed up, the lender is ticked and wonders if you didn't have them work this file to see what they would do. Sometimes even if there was a legitimate offer, the lender would insist that the file on the original be closed and the next offer is started from the beginning. **All** the way from the beginning.

The second method, which I prefer, is listing the shortsale at market value and then systematically lowering the price about 2% per week every week (or 5% every two weeks) until you have a legitimate offer from a buyer with a pre-qualifying letter, a pre-approval letter, or proof of funds. (if it is a cash transaction) This method works wonders because you will be submitting to the bank the property listing history. They will see firsthand how you started out at a regular price but with no one even looking, the price had to be dropped and dropped until you were finally able to get an offer. This also helps the BPO (Broker Price Opinion person justify a low estimate because the market has spoken. With this method, everything is aboveboard and open.

Taking into account exactly how much time the average shortsale takes, you yourself have to figure out how many shortsale listings you can comfortably handle at one time. A lot will depend on how you schedule your time, how much of the activities you're going to do yourself, how motivated you are, etc. I say this because with competition being almost nil, and all the shortsale listing leads you can handle, you can have as many listings as you want. When I first started, I had virtually no money and knew no one, so did everything myself. I wrote up the brochures, printed them out, and then tri-folded them while I was on hold with the lender. I took the magnets and peeled off the tape and attached it to each card while I was on hold for the lender. I went to the online court records and the property tax records to get the LP's and NOD's while I was on hold with the lender, I hand addressed the envelopes of the letters I was sending out while on hold with the lenders. I ... well, you get the point. If you're the one making calls to the lenders, make sure that you have some mundane task that needs to be done, yet takes very little concentration. Do it while you're on hold.

One last thing about honesty with the homeowner concerning the listing. Do not guarantee anything. Yes, you can put a price low enough that you should get offers no matter how bad the market is. That doesn't guarantee a sale. Nothing does. Despite what advertisers have led us to believe, there are no guarantees in life. I saw one of the scammer postcards of a homeowner that had actually signed over the deed to his house and power of attorney. When I asked the homeowner why he would do such a thing, he pointed to the card and said, "see, right there, it says, '*guaranteed* to stop foreclosure.'"

Chapter Four

The Shortsale Package

There is nothing more important than the shortsale package. An incomplete, outdated, wrong information, not labeled shortsale package is the number one reason the average Realtor fails at shortsales. You will do it right and it will be the number one reason you succeed. All pages of the shortsale package will be put in the appendix.

As I mentioned in the previous chapter, the first and most important document you need and that you should have signed right at the listing appointment is the Letter of Authorization. This will be the absolute first thing you send to a lender. Some lenders have separate fax lines for authorization letters and shortsale packages. Make sure you send the right thing to the right fax number and always send the Letter of Authorization separate AND before the shortsale package. Without this initial Authorization letter, the lender is prohibited by law from discussing any aspect of the loan with you.

The Authorization Letter

The authorization letter should include the sellers' full name, address of the property, loan number, last four digits of the social security #'s, full names printed and signed, and the people that the authorization is for. This should include yourself, the name of the closing agent at the title company that you will have open title on the property, (more on this later) and anyone that is going to be calling the lender to work the shortsale. For example, an assistant or if you're in an office that has a "calling shortsale lender person," or if you decide to farm out (outsource) the calling the lenders thing, you would need the name of that person or organization. You also should have the name of the real estate company you're working for with your cell, fax, and regular office phone and an e-mail.

After the authorization is faxed, you can work on getting a complete shortsale package put together while you're waiting for an offer to come in on the property. Some people will tell you that the order of the pages is important but I think this is only true concerning a document like a purchase offer. It is multiple pages and you really should take the trouble to make sure page 2 follows page 1 and so on.

The Client Financial Worksheet

The client financial worksheet normally can be a generic type sheet like the one included in the appendix or occasionally the lender has their own specific form. ASC which is the loan servicer for Wells Fargo is one of these. One company refused my form and insisted I transfer all the data to their particular form with the seller signing the "new" form. What was the difference in the forms? Their form had the Lender letterhead at the top. Otherwise the two forms were identical!

The financial worksheet gives the lender some idea of the clients financial situation. If the worksheet shows that if they tightened up their budget a notch, the owner actually *could* afford the house, then the lender *may* offer a loan modification. If the worksheet shows the owner *cannot* afford the house, the lender will go ahead and (99.9% of the time) do a short sale. If the owner can probably pay or has significant assets, the lender will probably head for foreclosure if the owner refuses a loan mod. This is to take back the property, file the deficiency judgement, and come after the homeowner for the difference. The financial statement is very important to the process and the numbers for expenses (groceries, utilities, cable, water, autos, gas, etc. should be in within reason. A lender will not check the statements of expenses with a private investigator but if the expenses seem unreasonably high, the lender will assume the homeowner is being deceitful and may deny the shortsale on those grounds. The bottom line is that the outgo must exceed the income by a significant amount. This is an amount that no reasonable budget restrictions can overcome.

The Hardship Letter

Another key factor that, strangely enough, is given a lot of weight by some lenders and isn't even considered by others is the Hardship letter. This is an explanation of hardship that is normally handwritten, signed, and dated. The letter basically gives a reason or excuse to the lender on exactly why they are late or totally unable to make their payments. "My house isn't worth what I paid for it" is not a valid excuse. Reasonable and valid excuses are something along the lines of, divorce, death, disaster, disease, destruction, and the main one lately is de-employment. (loss of job)

The exception to the handwritten part is when the owner's handwriting is totally ineligible or read with great difficulty, and illiteracy. In both cases, I normally type out what the homeowner says is the reason for the hardship, let them read it or I read it back to them, and then have it signed and dated. The hardship letter must ALWAYS be signed and dated no matter what form it's written in.

If available, it's also a good idea to include a paper trail concerning the hardship. This could be: hospital bills, repair bills, divorce decree, letter of termination or "pink slip" or any supporting documentation for information in the hardship letter. Make sure the times coincide. For example, if you cite divorce as the reason for the hardship, the divorce decree better not be 5 years old. If a car accident, 5 year old hospital bills won't help much.

Two Most Recent Month Bank Statements

The 2 most recent months' checking account is next on the list of documents needed for the complete shortsale package. This gives the lender an idea of how much money is coming in and how much is going out and what the money is going for and how much is accumulating. (if any) Just as they wanted corroborating paper evidence for the hardship letter, this is paper corroboration of the client financial sheet.

Two Most recent Pay Stubs

When you give copies to the lender of your 2 most recent paystubs, this is reinforcement again of the client financial statement. Take home monthly income is stated on the financial sheet and it needs to match up pretty closely with the pay stubs. Some homeowners are receiving unemployment income. Even though this is temporary, the lender still wants that income counted. With a regular paycheck that is direct deposited, the employer also sends a paper trail to the employee stating how much money was deposited and where it went. It is fine to include these statements in lieu of actual pay stubs. If the unemployed have direct deposit they are **not** sent a paper trail and have no proof of how much the income is directly. Indirectly, if the homeowner will circle the direct deposit amounts on the 2 months bank statements with a notation about what it is, that is acceptable.

Last Two Years Tax Returns

Now for the final back up documentation of the client financial form, the lender wants the last 2 years tax returns from the homeowner. Just one year back is sufficient most of the time depending on what time of the year it is. For documentation of documentation of documentation they also ask that the w-2's for the homeowner/employee be included. The good news is that they really are only interested in the top 3 pages of the tax return so you don't have to send the entire return.

In the case of the self-employed, the lender sometimes wants to see a profit and loss statement for at least the past fiscal year and sometimes likes to see the quarterly tax contributions. As an independent contractor, we Realtors walk a fine line between employee and independent business. The tax return and sometimes the lender will tell you if they need additional information.

Divorce Decree

A divorce decree *must* be included if it is part of the hardship and it *must* be included if the property was bought while the couple was married. It doesn't matter if either person bought the property as a sole owner. If the sole owner was married when they bought property the Title Company that is guaranteeing or insuring *clear* Title to the property must make certain there can be no future claims of any interest in the property. If a person was divorced 5 years ago and got their final decree at that time and *then* went and bought a house, the divorce decree would be unnecessary as there would be no possible legal interest in the house

The Last Payment Coupon From the Lender

This serves 2 purposes. One, is for you to verify the exact loan number and who the actual lender or servicer is. The second reason is to give you an approximate payoff amount on the lien. The payoff amount isn't that important if there is only the one first mortgage. If there is a second lien holder, the payoff amount is very important as the first mortgage lender will determine how much they will allow the second lien holder to receive.

Before shortsales were so prevalent, the first lien holder would normally give the second lien holder $1,000 as a "take it or leave it." If the property went to foreclosure, the second lien holder would receive nothing *except* the right to *also* file a deficiency judgment against the homeowner. With shortsales becoming more and more common, the second lien holder has *some* power because the title company cannot proceed without the written approval of *all* lien holders. This is what happens:

The first lien holder estimates they will save $25,000 by doing a shortsale rather than foreclosing. There is a second lien for $50,000. The second lien holder says to the first lien holder, unless we get $5,000 we won't agree to remove our lien. This amount happens to fall within the guidelines of the lender reluctantly agreeing to what would be a no-brainer for average folks like you and me. The first lien lender is still coming out $20,000 ahead of a foreclosure sale. (but giving up their right to pursue for deficiency if the homeowner is insolvent) The second lien holder is getting $5,000 they normally wouldn't have and they *almost* always give up their rights to pursue a deficiency also.

Even if the homeowner is insolvent, the second lien holder will sometimes ask for a deficiency note to be signed. Using the example of a $50,000 debt to the second and a $50,000 deficiency to the first here's what could happen.

If foreclosed, the homeowner will have a judgment filed of $50,000 for the first and for 50,000 for the second. Nobody is happy. Especially you that did all the work and now aren't going to get paid. If it goes to shortsale, the first accepts the debt as settled and the second may file a deficiency for the remaining $45,000. Not good but not as bad as the full $50,000. The good is that you get paid. The ideal is that the first settles the second settles and you get paid. Everybody isn't happy maybe, but everyone is at least satisfied and you are happy. When these accounts are entered at the credit bureau, these entries usually read something along the lines of, "Account Settled. Not for Full Amount."

Signed Real Estate Listing Agreement

As mentioned in the chapter concerning listings, a signed listing agreement is a requirement of a shortsale. The bank wants to know that the home is being exposed to the greatest number of potential buyers since that is the only way to get the best price. One of the ways freelancers work is to get the owner to sign the deed over to him. He negotiates a shortsale with the lender for a certain price. Meanwhile they try to find a buyer to pay $20-30,000 more than the price they negotiated with the bank. Sometimes they are honest and actually have a Realtor list the house and sometimes they just use a fake listing. Some of the lenders are real strict about the listings. Make sure the listing is up to date, all the signatures are on it and all the initials. I had one lender told me my shortsale package would not be reviewed further until I put in MY missing *initials* on one of the three pages of the listing form!

Signed Purchase and Sale Agreement

Lenders have been so swamped with shortsales that they usually do not even consider a shortsale at all until there is already an offer on the table. A signed purchase and sale agreement is a key component of a complete shortsale package. The average Loss Mitigator is working with an average of 200 files at any given time. If you were a Loss Mitigator (LM from here on out) how much time would you spend on an incomplete file? Since an incomplete file has NO chance for success and there are plenty of complete files that the LM can work on, which files are going to get the bulk of the attention.

Since some lenders base compensation to the LM based on how many files they close out, will the LM spend much time with impossibilities? Why would they do extra work and try to educate the Rookie about shortsales when there are plenty of experienced Realtors sending packages from all over the country? Most LM's can glance through a file and tell if the person sending it in is totally inexperienced and/or knows anything about shortsales. They can also tell if the package was sent in by a pro. They have 4 stacks of files. Incoming (the files coming in each day) Outgoing (files being closed) Good (files that have a high probability of a successful closing) and Bad. (files that they'll get to if all the other work is taken care of)

Some successful Realtors prefer to submit a contract signed by both parties and some successful Realtors prefer to only have the buyer side signed. Both methods have their advantages and disadvantages. With both buyer and seller signed on the purchase offer, it becomes a contract and the listing must be pended. After pending the listing, it is unusual to get back up offers. Here is what can happen without a backup offer:

If the shortsale offer is denied or countered and the buyers will not or cannot come up, you may have to really scramble to find another buyer before foreclosure comes up. If the house is near the foreclosure sale date and there is an offer on the table that the lender is reviewing, the lender may postpone or cancel the sale. With no back up contract, they won't hesitate to go ahead and foreclose. Unfortunately, most lenders wait until the foreclosure sale is within the next 48 hours before they send a fax or e-mail to the agent set to bid for the property on their behalf.

If a home you have listed is scheduled for foreclosure, get any kind of offer in that you can. Drastically drop the price, get people looking, call agents and buyers that had looked at the house before at the higher price. The house may not have worked for them at that time but it's amazing how much difference a 25% price drop can do to an attitude about the house.

If you **don't** have the seller sign, you do not have to pend the listing, and you may get some back up offers. Make sure the seller is presented all offers that come in and make sure the Realtors bringing in back up offers is fully aware that there is an offer *before* their offer and that the first offer has first right of refusal. Many Realtors will get upset if the offer they have isn't first and you don't submit it to the bank. You kindly tell them that you aren't under legal obligation to submit their offer after it's been presented to the seller. Then point out that the first offer has first right of refusal because their offer was submitted first. Then politely explain that it has been your experience that submitting more than one shortsale offer at a time is very confusing to the lenders and it shuts down all progress. It's true the other Realtor may pull his buyers out when he hears the offer isn't even going to be submitted but he probably wouldn't have brought an offer at all if the listing had been pended.

Without pending a listing, buyers aren't required to put up a deposit. With no deposit, there is little motivation to stay if the value of the home keeps dropping, the buyers find a better house, the buyers are impatient, or if they decide it will just never happen with the shortsale on the house. That's what back ups are for.

When the listing is pended, the other Realtors understand their position, a deposit is taken, and the lender doesn't give any flack about why the seller hasn't signed the contract. Usually the lender doesn't care if the seller hasn't signed the contract until they get ready to approve it. Sometimes, however, the lender will demand the sellers' signature on the contract before they will even start the review process.

I look at it this way. If it's a good house in a good location at a good price, go ahead and pend the listing because back up offers will come in even with the listing in pending status. If the listing is a doghouse in a bad area and an offer comes in, go ahead and pend the listing because you'll probably never get another offer on the house anyway. So after trying it both ways, you may prefer one way over another, it's up to you. In either case, I NEVER put a "pending offer" on any for sale sign... It's like telling a potential buyer not to bother you with a phone call and to call someone else that DOESN"T have a "pending sale" on their sign.

Having the seller sign and pending the listing immediately as the contract is submitted for third party approval is successful. So is NOT having the seller sign the offer and submitting that offer within the shortsale package. Use what works for you in your area. Keep in mind that other realtors are your bread and butter so to speak if you concentrate on listings. The other realtors in your area bring you the buyers and you need to stay on good terms with all of them. Being "blacklisted" (other realtors refusing to show your property) can kill a listing career or force you to work with buyers. Working with buyers isn't easy to begin with, but you have the added complication of not knowing if the listing agent is competent to complete a shortsale.

The Hud-1

The HUD-1 is the document that basically tells the lender what the bottom line is. The exact amount to the penny they will net after all is said and done. Hopefully, the Title company your company works with or you will begin working with is experienced in shortsales. As the listing agent, you are working for the seller and the seller normally is required to demonstrate clear title or ownership to the property before it is sold. This is so the buyer will also have clear title and any liens or encumbrances against the property will be of his own doing and not that of the former owner. The hud-1 will be prepared for you free of charge by the title company you're planning to use for closing. They will "open title" which simply means they will do the preliminary title work and let you know if there are any possible surprises when it comes to the closing.

Once the lender has a pretty good idea what the net will be, they will decide if this amount is acceptable to them. This is why it is a good idea to "pad the hud." The title company fills out the hud according to your specifications. How much commission, how much in HOA (Home Owner Association) fees, how much is being offered to the second, your compliance or processing fee your property maintenance fee are all variables and most are known as "junk fees." Lenders don't always pay these fees but it never hurts to ask and they have surprised me sometimes when they have paid them. A lot depends on how much of a hit they are taking and how close the offer is to the BPO.

Lenders have guidelines. Lenders rarely have any idea of what a property is worth and depend almost entirely on the BPO. This can be good and bad since the BPO is normally not done by an actual appraiser but by another Realtor like yourself that may just be asked to do a "drive by appraisal." With the amounts of money involved, it surprises me that a lender will pay $40 bux for a drive by BPO instead of $350 bux for an actual certified appraiser to totally evaluate the property. If the BPO comes in too high, the property may end up being foreclosed due to no willing buyers and it will cost the bank maybe an extra $20k. If it comes in too low, then the bank will lose more than it would have with an accurate appraisal. Naturally, you want the BPO to come in as low as possible so that whatever offer you have is more likely to be acceptable.

The guidelines the lender has varies with each lender and for Fannie Mae and Freddie Mac backed loans. The average acceptable net for most lenders is around 18% less than whatever the BPO is. This figure includes ALL closing costs, Realtor commissions, and lien payoffs. There are always exceptions but based on those guidelines, you can see why the offer needs to come pretty close to the BPO. It is also why the second lien holder can and sometimes does mess up your deal.

I had a deal fall through once because the second lien holder demanded **80%** of the balance. The first was willing to give them a generous 10% (about 5k) but there was no way they would shell out almost 40 grand when foreclosure would wipe that second lien out completely. The sellers were mad at me for not stopping foreclosure but I called the lender three times and talked to the decision maker. Each time, the lender said that they would rather get nothing at foreclosure and pursue their legal rights against the homeowner than accept a "stinkin" 10% on a defaulted second. Go figure. They even had the gall to tell me I should reveal to them where the sellers had moved to so they could "get their money." This lender was the exception, so don't worry about it happening with any regularity.

Your Own BPO

It's not required but, it is a good idea to do your own BPO on the property. You will be more thorough than the person hired to whip in and out for a piddlin 50 bux. You will use all the low comparables. Find out absolutely everything that is wrong with the house and take pictures of the defects if possible. Find out the crime stats for the neighborhood, (the sheriff or city police dept. will be happy to supply you with that) find out where the nearest sexual predators are to the subject property and find out if the schools nearby have a bad rating or not. Put all this information together and put it in summary form in the shortsale package. Keep the larger file, make a copy and give the copy to the BPO person when you meet them for the BPO. Make sure to include pictures of every room inside a couple of front shots from different angles, a back shot, and a street shot. (the one that will show the junker up on blocks) Your mission, should you decide to accept it, is to get the BPO as absolutely low as you can possibly get it. This is one of the very most important things to getting a deal through as so much hinges on the BPO and its' relation to the offer. The BPO person simply won't have the time to do all that you did. Being on time constraints and being paid very little, it is not unusual to have the BPO person simply hand in your work and sign their name to it! Why not? It's thorough, it's accurate, and it's done. The fact that it will totally jive with the summary BPO you sent within the shortsale package will make everyone look good. Even the lender will be impressed at what a thorough job was done on the BPO.

MLS Price History

This is (obviously) a history of what prices you have had the property listed at. This is irrefutable evidence that the property was not worth the previously listed prices because no one looked at or made an offer at the higher prices. Here is an example:

Listed 10/27/08.........................$150000

Price change 11/11/08.............$146,000

Price change 11/25/08.............$142,000

Price change 12/10/08.............$138,000

Price change 12/26/08.............$134,000

Price change 01/10/09.............$130,000

Price change 01/25/09.............$126,000

Price change 02/09/09.............$122,000

Price change 02/24/09.............$119,000

This systematic reduction shows the lender that you gave buyers plenty of time to make an offer IF the price was competitive. If no offers came in, it shows that the house did not compare to other available homes that were on the market during this period of time in this price range. For a buyer to put up with the hoops that the lender puts them through and the time that they have to wait and all the stuff that goes on with even a regular shortsale, they need to have a much better deal than a "regular" house.

This is just my opinion, but in a declining market, a shortsale house is worth about 15% less than a comparable "regular" house. In a stable or slightly rising market, the shortsale is still worth about 8-10% less than a regular house. With a regular house, you can normally get a "yes" or "no" answer within 24 hours and the buyer can actually be living in the house within

45 days of the initial purchase offer. With a shortsale, it sometimes takes 45 days or more to even get a loss mitigator to be assigned to review your shortsale package. Many go over 90 days before a final decision is made and then all the sellers documentation needs to be updated. A BPO offer if only good for 90 days and I've dealt with some lenders that were so backlogged that the BPO had *also* expired! (more than once!)

Since a home is truly only worth what a ready, willing, able, and knowledgeable buyer is willing to pay, the listing history is prime evidence put up against an unreasonable BPO. An actual example: I *initially* listed a house at $176,000 and went through the price reductions similar to the example shown above, I got a full listing price offer when the listing price got down to $132,000.

Within 2 more weeks I got 2 back up offers also at $132,000. The BPO came back at $182,000!! I pleaded for another BPO to be done and sent in my low comps. The second BPO came back at $176,000!! What could I do? I sent the listing history with a re-emphasis on the homes defects and showing that even though the house might be worth the prices the 2 BPO's came in at, It wasn't worth that amount at this time in this market. The bank finally agreed to accept the $132,000. Interesting side note. Due to all the banks silliness and jerking around, the first buyer walked before they came back with acceptance, believing it would never happen. The second buyers had also walked, reasoning that even if the bank *did* come back at the $132k the first buyers would get the house. The third buyers ended up with the house!

Loan Numbers

This is crucial to everything that has anything to do with a shortsale package. Every scrap of paper that is e-mailed, faxed, snail mailed, hand delivered, etc. absolutely must, without fail, contain the loan numbers on it. The numbers must be large and easily readable. Get a stamp made up with the words, LOAN #_____ and fill in the blank. Sometimes you can get a gadget that will have nine *adjustable* numbers on it. This is perfect since it can be grueling to handwrite "Loan # and the loan number" on the approximate 22 pages that go into a typical shortsale package. I recommend that you e-mail the entire package to the LM as soon as one has been assigned which should also be sometime after the package has been faxed in. Occasionally, a lender is not very backed up and they will assign a loss mitigator just on the evidence of a potential shortsale. They know something's up when the authorization letter is sent in with the name of your real estate company on it.

Cover Page

Finally, in addition to the traditional fax cover page, send in an additional cover page. This *real* cover page will be like the Table of Contents in a book. With a sharpie pen, write the page number in the upper right hand corner of each page number. On the cover page, put what page each section starts at. For example, Borrowers Financial Statement page 3, purchase offer page 6, Hardship Letter on page 9...and so on whatever it is. In addition to the table of contents, give a brief summary of what the package is and contains and give the lender what the bottom line net is to them. Many LM's look at the first few pages and if the package looks like you know what you are doing and have been successfully doing it, they are more likely to pay attention to *your* package rather than dread having to deal with disorganized, incomplete packages sent in by other Realtors.

Loan # stamp

Chapter Five

Lenders and Loss Mitigators

When dealing with the lenders, you aren't actually dealing directly with the Lenders but actually the Loss Mitigators. The Loss Mitigators are paid to follow the guidelines set by the Lenders and can only rarely get permission to make exceptions.

Foreclosures happen in all 50 states. Some of these states are Judicial Foreclosure states. The rest are not. Both have advantages and disadvantages. In a judicial foreclosure state, the homeowner typically has several months to stay in the home without making payments as the wheels of justice grind slowly and everything must be done following due process. The drawback is that if the property goes to foreclosure then the lender has a legal right to file a deficiency judgment. With a judicial judgment, the lender can pursue the former homeowner to the point of confiscation of bank accounts, wages, and any property of value owned. Not a pleasant thought.

In a non-judicial foreclosure state, the home can be foreclosed and the homeowner expected to be totally moved out within 21 days of official notice of default. That is extremely fast, but the homeowner has an advantage. No matter how much the difference was between what was owed on the home and what the home sold for at auction, the lender does **not** have the right to pursue the former homeowner for any of the money. None. They're done. The lender probably won't be lending any money to the homeowner in the near future but hey, at least the lender won't be chasing after their assets.

In almost all loss mitigation departments, the lender has flunkies. A flunkie is someone that is paid very little, knows very little and has very little say-so on your deal. Their main job is to keep you from "bothering" the loss mitigator with questions that they themselves can answer. Most information on your deal is uploaded to an "accessible by associated parties" file. This is a good system in some respects. As long as all information is uploaded properly and the LM inputs requirements, it works. The problem is that the average LM is working with anywhere between 150-250 files at any given time. If they get about 10 new files a day, that means they have to "close out" about 10 files a day just to stay even with the workload they have.

I'm going to ask you to think like an overworked, underpaid, loss mitigator for a moment. You receive a file that is missing a lot of required documents. It looks like the person that put the file together didn't have the slightest idea of what they were doing. Are you going to waste time even looking at the file further or will you put it at the bottom of the priority heap?

Now, you get a file that has all the required documents, everything is done properly and it looks like the person that put the file together looks like they have done this plenty of times before and even include additional helpful information. Do you put this at the top of the pile to look at further and immediately order a BPO? Of course, and this is what typically happens every day. It's not your job as a loss mitigator to educate people on proper procedure for submitting the shortsale package so why waste time on something that will probably not work because of an incomplete file?

The LM has a quota they must meet every month concerning how many of these houses in the shortsale process they bring to successful conclusion so they are naturally going to "work" the files that have the best chance of success. This is why it is pointless to submit a file that does not include a purchase offer. Would YOU waste your time on a file that may never have an offer on it when you have over 100 that do?

When calling the LM, you will very rarely actually get a hold of the LM directly. It is important to document all your calls and get the names of the people you talk to. Be very friendly and always go in to the call with an attitude of "Please help me help you." Getting angry or belligerent never helps the situation and it is possible that a bad attitude will get you "blacklisted." By blacklisted, it means that you will have offended one or more people to the extent that your name gets passed around to the other flunkies and they make sure your file gets put on the bottom of huge stacks of files... or lost!

Documenting all your calls is simply a matter of recording when you called, what file you called on, who you talked to and what action was taken. This will be extremely helpful for you so that you don't have to remember everything that is going on with 20+ listings you will be carrying. When someone calls you for an update, you can quickly pull out the latest update sheet and relay exactly what happened. Sometimes I simply copy the update and e-mail it to the buyers' agent. This way they can e-mail it on to their inquisitive and "antsy" buyers so that they know that "something's being done." It also gives them something "in writing" so everything they hear isn't word of mouth. Word of mouth sometimes comes across as rumor and verbal messages sometimes get garbled.

Another reason to document all your calls is that when you call in, the flunkies will tell you they need this or that document. When you tell them you have already faxed that document, they will want to know when. If you say something like, "Oh, about a week or so ago" it doesn't have nearly the impact of, "That document was faxed to ASC (or whatever the lender is) at 2:30 PM on June 12th." They will then ask you the most important thing about sending documents to these lenders or loan servicers.

"Was the correct loan number put on the documents you faxed?" EVERY single scrap of paper that you fax to a lender MUST have the correct loan number on it. Not just the top page, not just the cover page, not just the first page of a 3 or 4 page contract, but EVERY page no matter how big or small. This **one mistake** alone is responsible for the majority of shortsales being worked to fall through. The reason is that any page that does not have the loan number on it WILL be lost or discarded and that will make the shortsale package incomplete and THAT will always get the deal turned down unless the LM feels sorry for you and gives you 48 hours to fax all the missing docs to them with the proper loan number on them.

Many of the lenders you will deal with are not actually lenders but servicers. They are not the actual people that lent the money but they are collecting the monthly mortgage, taking a small service fee, and handling loss mitigation or short sales. This is the reason there are sometimes different names between who filed the Lis Pendens, Notice of Default, or foreclosure proceedings and who the homeowner has been making the monthly payment to. This is especially true if the loan has been assigned and it's not unusual for a loan to get assigned (sold) once it goes into default. Sometimes the actual lender will have their own loss mitigation department and sometimes there is even a separate entity altogether to handle everything. This also occurs when the loan has been sold.

Usually, a second lien holder will try to dump or sell their position to another party when the loan defaults. The reason for this is, if no shortsale is done on the property, the house is almost always foreclosed. In the event the house is foreclosed, **ALL liens** are *wiped off* the books and the highest bidder at the auction is the sole owner of the property. If only $100k is owed on the house, the house is worth $200k, and there is only a second mortgage of $20k, then the second lien holder would be better off to outbid the first lien holder and get the house sold so they can also get compensated for the $20k they have invested. Even a quick sale of the $200k valued property at $150 would cover all the money invested and the second would get the $100k they paid the first AND the $20k that was owed them on the second.

Unfortunately, what has been happening in the current market is almost the opposite of the above example. Now we have a house with a first lien of $150k. There is a second lien of $37k, (an 80/20 - 100% loan) and the home is currently worth maybe $110k. The first lien holder is going to lose a ton of money no matter what happens. The second lien holder is going to lose a ton of money no matter what happens. Make no mistake, even in a shortsale, both lien holders lose quite a bit. The point is that they don't lose as much as they normally would have if the property had gone all the way to foreclosure.

In the above scenario, the first lien holder would lose about $90k if the property went to foreclosure. $150k-$30k for the cost of foreclosing, then selling the $110k house for $100k, then paying out about $10k (10%) for closing costs, real estate commissions and miscellaneous expenditures (HOA, maintenance, property tax, insurance, etc.) This brings the total net to the lender at about $90k and does not count the cost of the foreclosure itself which generally runs about $30-40k.

When looking at the Hud-1 statement that ALWAYS, MUST, be included along with each purchase offer, the lender is most concerned with the bottom line. The bottom line for the lender is exactly how much money the lender is going to net after all is said and done. The actual amount of the check that is being wired to the lender after closing. The hardship letter can be the best in the world, the bank statements can reflect the seller is dirt poor, and the seller can be unemployed with a ton of credit card debt. None of that really matters if the net to the lender isn't within certain guidelines relating to the BPO or the comparables.

Listing agents and selling agents are both in this business for the fee or commissions earned. Naturally, this is the first point that Lenders work on to increase the net to them. They will ask you to cut your commission. They will say it is their policy. They will say they are not permitted to pay more than "X%." This is something you will have to work out. Yes, the president said that lenders must pay full (reasonable) commission. Part of the way lenders get around that is to have a loss mitigation company take care of this nasty little business for them. For example, in my area, at this time, some realtors charge 6% commission. The standard cut is to 5% if there are 2 realtors involved and 4% if you have both the buyer and seller as a transaction broker. Makes you want to take your buyers to a regular listing or someone else's shortsale listing so you'll be paid more. What is entirely stupid is if the lender is willing to pay 5% when 2 different realtors are involved but won't pay you 5% if the whole deal is yours. It's like they don't think you've *earned* all you did if you do both sides at once instead of at different times. Sometimes it just boils down to that they don't like seeing any one person make a good chunk of change on a transaction that they are losing so much on.

One way to make up for this loss of commission is to put on some add-on fees or "junk fees." A compliance fee can sometimes be put in for around $250 and sometimes they will accept a maintenance fee of around $250. Another possibility is a $495 negotiating fee as the banks realize there is much more work involved in a shortsale. It's kind of like admitting that they know they've been jerks to work with. I never ask the sellers or buyers to pay any of these fees. I always ask the lender to pay these fees although I know that some brokers are getting the buyer to pay some of these fees. Again, a lot of this stuff depends on how close the offer is to the BPO.

Depending on the bottom line net to the lender, they are sometimes willing to pay buyer concessions. A concession is the lender paying all or part of the buyers closing costs. Sometimes these costs are put into the purchase offer to increase the net to the lender. They give more with the offer but take it back away with the concessions. A lot of buyers just don't have a lot of cash to put down and sticking the closing costs into the mortgage works for a lot of people. Sometimes the closing costs exceed the down payment!

Multiple offers occur on a property that is usually a good deal. If the property is priced low enough, you can get plenty of offers but the problem happens when the BPO comes in way higher than list price. The lender *has* to net out a certain percentage of whatever the BPO is and a high BPO will kill a deal in a minute. Another problem you may encounter is the lender tells you how much they have to net. Your buyer offered a price that will give them that net, BUT...the buyer has no money for closing costs and must put it into the purchase price and have it come back out from the lender. Now, will the new buyers lender appraise the property high enough to cover the closing costs?

Many brokers handle multiple offers differently. One way is to put in a "dummy" offer that is extremely low. The broker doesn't expect the offer to be accepted but it does "get the ball rolling" so to speak in the sense that a BPO gets ordered and a loss mitigator assigned. The Realtor maybe has the property listed for $150k. The fake offer is submitted for $75k. Meanwhile, the realtor tries to get a legitimate offer on the property. The lender comes back and says, "we've crunched the numbers and there is no way we can accept the $75k offer. If you can get the buyer up to $110k then we can work a deal." While the lender was trying to decide on the $75k offer, A legitimate offer of $112k came in. The realtor responds back to the lender, "That first offer buyer won't come up to the $110 but I've got great news! Another buyer just put another offer in for $112k and we're good to go. I'll fax the new offer and hud with the pre-qual letter today."

First of all, an offer like that is deceptive and therefore unethical. Second, the lender doesn't take kindly to wasting their limited resources to look at dummy offers. Third, it's possible that you won't get a legitimate offer until the file has been closed on the first offer (which means a new loss mitigator) or the BPO is more than 90 days old. (which means a new BPO) Fourth, all the paperwork from the seller may need to be updated by this time. Fifth, sometimes the defaulted loan is sometimes sold to another company. I actually had a shortsale that I was promised verbally shortsale approval on and when I called about the written approval, I was told the loan had been bundled and sold to another investor. Fortunately the new investor accepted the original price but the whole process was delayed about 40 days.

Another way to handle multiple offers is to get a legitimate offer but **not** have the seller sign which keeps it from being a legal contract. The listing does not have to be pended and the lender usually only asks for the offer to be signed by the seller if they are going to approve it. This enables multiple offers to come in. The problem with this is the 2nd or 3rd offer gets upset if **their** offer isn't also presented to the lender. (especially if it's higher) and **if** you **do** present a second offer, the lender gets totally confused. Always remember that the lender simply cannot evaluate more than one offer at a time. Another problem is that the buyer doesn't have to put down a deposit since there is no contract and the listing isn't pended. Once you have 3rd party approval, have the seller sign the offer making it a contract, pend the listing, and get the deposit

After trying the previous 2 methods, I am now doing my shortsales like this: I list the property at 5-10% below market value and then regularly drop the price until I get a legitimate offer on it. Then I have the seller sign the offer, pend the listing and get the deposit from the buyers. Make sure you put in the pended listing that you are taking backups. This way, there is a spiraling downward listing history, the whole process is legitimate, and other realtors won't get mad at you thinking there were no other offers before theirs on the property.

As with multiple offers on a property, there are additional problems with multiple liens. If there is a second lien holder (and there usually is) then you will need to submit the same paperwork to the second lien holder that was submitted to the first. The only difference might be the hud. On the hud to the first, you may show a payoff of $3-5k. On the hud to the second, you may show a payoff of only $1,000. There is a reason for this. Everyone wants more. The first lien holder wants the highest net to them in their pocket. They want to give as little as possible to anyone else and that includes you, your commission, and any second lien holder. The advantage to you is that even if they foreclose, they will still have to pay a commission and the usual closing costs. If they foreclose, they don't have to pay anything at all to the second lien holder.

The second lien holder used to just quietly take a token $1,000 for their position as second. Those days are almost gone. Since more and more shortsales are cropping up, the second lien holder is realizing they have some say in the matter. After all, the shortsale is not possible without their agreement. Yes, if the property foreclosed they would receive nothing, but they would retain their rights to pursue a deficiency judgment and may recoup some money in the future. The whole idea of a shortsale is that the lender is almost always surrendering any rights to further pursuit on the deficiency. (The deficiency is what is owed minus what the property sells for) By accepting a shortsale, all lien holders are pretty much agreeing to drop the matter at the point of sale. This usually shows up on the credit report with something along the line of, "Account settled, but not for full amount, or, Account settled, but not according to agreement." Also, "Account settled not according to agreement and not for full amount." "Account settled" is the key.

Second lien holders have a bag of lies that they will tell the Realtor to try to get more money. I've had them tell me that they have 2nd lien insurance which will pay them 20% if the loan forecloses and they therefore must have 20% of their loan on a shortsale. According to loss mitigators I've come to know quite well that handle first and second mortgages, there is **no** such thing as 2nd mortgage insurance. I've even had second lien holders tell me that they will approve the money offered to them on the hud but that their policy will not let me, as a realtor, receive any more than 4% total commission. This is baloney. They do not have any say in how much commission my office is to receive since it is determined by the first lien holder and I've told them so.

If there are other liens or judgments against the property besides the first and second you will have additional "challenging opportunities (problems) to show your skills and elevate you to peak performance." If there are other judgments or liens, these also need to be removed to enable the first lien holder to give clear title without foreclosing. I.R.S. liens can sometimes be removed with the understanding that they are not relinquishing their rights to squeeze every drop of blood they can out of your sellers after the deal is done. It isn't easy. Other liens and judgments can sometimes be bought out for pennies on the dollar since they will normally be left with nothing and no other property to attach. The first lien holder won't do it, the second lien holder won't do it, the sellers almost never will do it, so I have occasionally had the minor lien holder or judgment holders paid out of my commission just to get the deal done. After a few of these, you will practically jump for joy when there are no judgments, no mechanics liens, no minor liens, no I.R.S. attachments and no second liens on the property. Sometimes this stuff shows up in the court records and when there are more than one or two items besides the first lien, I don't waste my time pursuing it. There are always plenty more leads with many fewer problems. Pursue the single mortgage sellers and it will go much easier for you. If there is ONLY a second lien, these are also worth pursuing. Homes with huge second mortgages can also be quite profitable – and not just the commission aspect. Here is a "secret" technique I learned by buying a "real estate guru's" book for only $40.

Find a home that is worth maybe $220k. There is a first of $140k and a second of $80k. The homeowner is behind 3 payments and bringing the FIRST mortgage current will take about $6k. (counting late and attorney fees) The homeowner wants to sell due to job loss, divorce, or whatever to help his credit somewhat. Tell the second lien holder that the property is headed for foreclosure and would they sell the second lien for 5% or $4k? Sometimes they will and sometimes they won't. Suppose they want $8k. For a total of 14k investment, you can buy the home for about $154k total. ($140k + $6k to bring current + $8K to buy out second lien= $154k) You now have a home worth $220k that you owe $154k on. You want a quick sale so you drop the price to $199k and pay closing cost of about 10% or $20k. This leaves you with a profit of $25k **not including** *the 3% or 6% real estate commission returned to you for listing and possibly selling your own house. Even only 3% will put your profit at over $30k total and shouldn't take more than about 20 hours* **total** *of your time. Not too many people earn* **$1500 per hour!** *Save up front costs by getting the first mtg. holder to do a loan mod, a forbearance or even a loan balance reduction.*

Something else to be aware of is that this is a "lender specific" business. Each lender has different rules and guidelines. Some are easy to work with and some are almost impossible. All lenders will accept the basic paperwork I've outlined in this book with minor variations. A few will require a particular form (like the financial form) be filled out on their particular stationary. At times,

I have had the lender request I put the information on the particular form they have faxed or e-mailed me, only to find it is identical to **MY** form except for *that* lenders, letterhead or logo. This is one of the typical hoops that lenders like to have you jump through on your way to a successful shortsale. Be glad! It's stuff like this that keeps other Realtors away from even attempting these deals ... or giving up when the going gets hard.

You should also be aware that the lender is not always the lender. By that, I mean that quite often the "lender" is merely the servicer. They aren't the money behind the loan. The servicer collects the payments each month and sometimes is actually the one that files the **Lis Pendens** or the **Notice of Default.** Both these terms mean the same thing, it's just a matter of what state your selling real estate in.

Basically, lis pendens is Latin for "lawsuit pending." Notice of default is makes the homeowner aware that the lender is beginning legal proceedings to recover the property that was used as security for the note. In a bankruptcy, if you don't make your payments on your car or truck, it WILL be repossessed regardless of whether or not it was listed in the bankruptcy filing. In the same way, the house WILL be repossessed if payments are not made regardless of whether or not it is listed in the bankruptcy.

So the lender is sometimes not actually the lender but is merely the servicer. Almost all loans are sold either individually or "bundled" and sold to entities like Fannie Mae or Freddie Mac.

Mortgage brokers are always working for lenders like Chase or Citibank and the loans are often actually through these companies and then sold. The servicer receives a small amount for servicing the loan but make it up by huge volume. About 50% of all loans are sold to Fannie Mae or Freddie Mac but they do not service these loans at all.

Loans also get sold when the homeowner is late on a payment since this is a sign of potential trouble. If the loan goes into default it is sold for a percentage of the total based on the payment history. Second mortgages that go into default are often sold for 10 cents on the dollar and fortunes have been made in the past by companies buying these discounted mortgages, filing deficiency judgments for the full amount and eventually recouping 2-3 times their initial investment.

Even though the lender is the "third party," the investor is the 4th party that is sometimes needed for approval. They can and do screw up perfectly good deals. The main way the investor will screw up the deal is to approve the loan with the condition that the homeowner/seller sign a note. I've seen them ask for anywhere between $5k and $35k. Sometimes the homeowner is willing to do this, sometimes not. This request from the investor is most often made when it is clear that the homeowner has some extra cash or if the homeowner currently owns and lives in another home. (especially if the home the seller is living in is NOT under foreclosure. The note they are asked to sign for is usually interest free and is always unsecured. Some homeowners take advantage of this and go ahead and sign. They then list that debt when they file for bankruptcy and it is wiped out in a successful bankruptcy.

How big is the average caseload of the average loss mitigator? As with almost everything, it depends on other factors. In the boom years, some loss mitigators were working as few as 10-12 cases nationwide. Some loss mitigators currently only have 30-40 case at any given time but they are also expected to answer the phone and assist with customer care. One company, The Loan Resolution Center has a general toll free number to call and about half the time I've called, the Loss mitigator working my file answered the phone.

Any Realtor that has worked a shortsale with any of the larger companies knows that it is almost impossible to get your Loss Mitigator on the phone even when you have a direct phone number! The last case I worked with Countrywide/Bank of America, the L.M. told me she was currently working 438 cases! This is another reason that "the squeaky wheel gets the oil." You must call early, late, and often. I do the calling myself to stay directly on top with each of my files. That way when a seller asks me what progress we are making or the buyers agent calls to tell me their buyers are getting antsy for the fourth time, I can give them a direct answer. I call on Tuesdays and Fridays (Mondays are extremely busy) and I lump the lenders together. For example, if I have 5 Wells Fargo files, I call and when done with the first case, go on to the next until all 5 are completed. This saves a lot of time on hold and getting the run around which is now the norm for shortsales.

Working multiple cases also lets the lender know you know what you're doing. They simply do not have time to train every newbie about proper protocol and what papers are necessary and how the shortsale package should be presented. According to the lenders own statistics, 9 out of 10 short sales that aren't successful are due to mistakes made by the agent. It's also important to develop a good relationship with the loss mitigators. Tell them thank you for all their help and tell them thank you for their time and tell them they are overworked (because they are) and tell them they are doing a job that you yourself couldn't possibly do. I think if I'm going nuts working 40 listings, how hard would it be to have 400 case files to work each month?

The important thing with Loss Mitigator relationships is to be the breath of fresh air in their day. Don't waste their time. Be organized. Be polite and courteous. Let the other Realtors yell at them, call them names and tell them they are stupid and see how successful they are. I have actually heard another Realtor say all these things so don't be surprised that it happens. Lenders have a "blacklist" and if your name gets on it whether with Chase or Countrywide or any of the other lenders, your name will be mud with that lender and you will have a tough time getting anything through. Find out the way each Loss Mitigator prefers to be contacted. Some prefer phone calls, some e-mails, and some by fax. Ask your loss mitigator on each case how they would prefer to be contacted. Make a note of it and then contact them in this way. Every time you talk to a person, make sure they give you their full name. Always keep track of what you did, when you did it and who did you talk to. For example, you call up a lender that you have called several times before on this same file. They say to you, "I'm sorry but we don't seem to have authorization to speak to you." When you answer, " I faxed the authorization over to you on March 27th at 3:15 P.M. EST and Janice Waters confirmed receipt of that fax on April 1st at 2:20 PM EST. The number I faxed it to was 866-555-8888." Trust me, that works 100 times better than when they asked me that same question when I was just starting out and I'd say, "Well, I'm not sure what number I faxed it to, but I know I faxed it a month or so ago."

You must always follow up to make sure they got everything that you send. When you send a shortsale package, make sure every scrap of paper you send over has the loan number on it. When they confirm they have received the shortsale package and assigned it to a loss mitigator, make sure that the loss mitigator does not need anything further concerning the package. If the package is not complete, it will get ignored. If you were a loss mitigator and had to be successful with a certain number of files each month, would you work the files that were complete and clean and the agent contacted you regularly to make sure you had everything you needed? Or would you work the barely legible, stuff missing files where it is sent in and nobody calls you to inquire about it? You can't go wrong if you think of things from the other person's point of view.

Chapter Six

The BPO or Appraisal

The BPO stands for **B**roker **P**rice **O**pinion. It is somewhat like an appraisal. A true appraisal is done by an actual professional that takes courses and practices under a master appraiser until they receive their certification. Appraising property is an art and there are good appraisers and bad appraisers. The good thing about appraisers is that you will rarely have to deal with them because a professional appraisal can run $250-450 dollars per house. A normal bank doesn't mind paying their CEO several million dollars to run the company into the ground, but when it comes to taking back houses, any expenditure on their part is a disaster.

This is where the BPO comes in. Rather than paying an actual appraiser about $350 for an actual appraisal, the bank goes on the cheap and gets a Realtor to give an opinion of what they feel the home is worth. There are two types of BPO's. There is the "drive by" BPO and there is the "interior" BPO. A drive by usually pays 35 to 40 dollars and an interior can pay between 50 and 75. Some brokers spend 3-4 hours doing one BPO. Some spend as little as 20 minutes. I had a BPO done on one of my properties today and the BPO person was in and out of the house in less than 60 seconds. Some spend no time at all and have an assistant drive out to the property, take the photos, and work up the BPO.

The assistant is usually unlicensed and gets about half what the lender is paying the broker. Some brokers make excellent money doing this by having many, many BPO's to do and having one or more assistants doing all the work.

The BPO is, by far, what will make or break your shortsale.

The reason is due to the fact that if the BPO comes in too high, it will be a miracle if an uneducated investor comes along and pays top dollar for what is clearly **not** a top dollar situation (A distressed property) The distressed property is on a timeline and once headed for foreclosure, it is rarely stopped and hardly ever slowed down. BPO's are good, or valid, for a period of 90 days. This is why it is crucial to get one as low as possible and as quickly as possible. I actually had to wait through 2 outrageous BPO's (180 days) by brokers that didn't even live or work in my area until the third one was accurate and the lender jumped at the same offer that they had sneered at previously.

I cannot stress the importance of meeting the BPO person at the house and doing the reverse of a buyer. Point out every possible thing you can that is wrong with the house and talk about the other factors that influence a homes value that are somewhat intangible.

What are some of the intangibles? Since some of the *tangibles* are a leaking or sagging roof, a cracked foundation, rotted fascia boards, termite damage, holes in the walls, and things along that nature. Some of the intangibles would be sexual predators living within half a mile of the subject property, only one bathroom, weird colors painted on the walls, extra high property taxes, extremely high and required homeowner association fees, and vacant houses in the area. Every vacant or foreclosed home within a half mile of the subject property will cause a 1% drop in perceived value of the home.

Your mission, should you choose to be successful at shortsales, is to make friends with the BPO person. Tell them the homeowners sad story so empathy will be felt. Explain that hardly anyone was even looking at the house when you were surprised to get even the offer you got. Tell them you need the BPO to come in as close to the purchase offer as they can reasonably make it so that your poor homeowners can finally get this nightmare of potential foreclosure behind them. Show them all the bad tangibles and talk about all the bad intangibles. Mention how bad the landscaping is (cuz it usually is) and how much it would reasonably cost to do all the repairs and fixing up that this house needs. Tell them your homeowners would have taken better care but it's about all they can do to keep the lights on and put food on the table. (I've used the previous things to tell the BPO person as examples. Do NOT EVER tell the BPO person something that is NOT true.)

The same goes for the buyers. The buyers are this young couple just starting out and they are willing to do the fixing up necessary with a little sweat equity but they are trying to be careful about overextending themselves and are so afraid of this economy and the perilous economic times we are facing that if there offer isn't accepted they just can't come up anymore and will have to keep renting until the situation for them specifically and the economy in general improves. Whatever truth you tell your new BPO friend, weave it as a story and paint a picture. Facts are just cold words that are soon forgotten. The picture you paint will stay with them and if they like you and feel empathy for the sellers, they will do their best to bring you that BPO price you are looking for.

I'm going to take a little break here and stop talking about shortsales for just a brief paragraph or two to give you information which may totally transform you and your salesmanship. Practice what I'm about to tell you and other people will love you, they will trust you, and they will look on you as a friend.

First, don't talk about yourself. Your plans, your dreams, your hopes, your goals, your likes and dislikes, your problems, your successes or failures. Except for you and possibly immediate family, nobody cares. The sellers you talk to that are forced to do a short sale because they have fallen on hard times do not care about your situation and need a sympathetic ear.

Second, let them do most of the talking and make sure it's about them. When you DO talk, make sure it's a question about them or to tell them you feel (if you really do) the same as they do about striped bass or the Dallas Cowboys or Boston Harbor or whatever it is that interests them. Everyone has a story to tell and if you let them tell you THEIR story, nodding and showing interest and asking questions like, "What did you do next?" or "How did that make you feel?" or "Why would they have done that to you?" you will have a new friend.

Other things that make the other person feel your empathy are phrases like, "Life isn't fair...you deserve better", "Bad things happen to good people like yourself", and "I'll do everything I can to help you through this and make it as painless as possible."... If you can't say those words (or similar) with honest sincerity and mean it with 99% of the people you do business with, you should quit this business. People do not care how much you know... they want to know how much you care. Sometimes you will be the only person they have any real contact with and the only person they can talk to that will truly listen to them. Once you learn you're in the people business first, foremost, and always, you'll be a success. I'm not saying be a friendly ignoramus. I just told you all you need to know about being a friend and having other people like you so you've got that part knocked. Now spend the next few years learning everything you can about real estate, your chosen profession. Ready? Get set...grow!!

Okay, back to shortsales and BPO's.

When you meet the BPO person, bring all the low comps you can and pictures of every room and everything that's wrong. If you know how to do a BPO (this is easily learned with free directions on the internet) do a complete BPO with adjustments and reasoning's and 30, 60, and 90 day projections. Give this directly to the BPO person and say, "This info I dug up may help you to arrive at a reasonable number. Feel free to use it however you want."... You'd be surprised how many people will take your work put their name on it and send it in. This is great. You've gotten the lowest reasonable number you can possibly get if this happens. You win, the BPO person wins, the bank wins, the buyers win, the sellers win, the Title company wins, the new lender wins, the new mtg. broker wins, the property tax people win, the HOA wins, the surveyors win, the other homeowners in the neighborhood win, the bank's appraisers win, and on and on.

The BPO is the key that unlocks benefits for everyone. A BPO that comes in unrealistically high will kill the deal and everyone loses. The BPO person MUST know what number you are shooting for or they may kill the deal. Make sure you form at least a minimal relationship with them. They aren't supposed to tell you what number they come up with but if you build a rapport with them they rarely will tell you right there but may give you a card so you can call them a few days later. If you do a lot of shortsales, you will be getting "repeaters" that have done BPO's on your listings in the past. Always be friendly, helpful, and professional.

Chapter Seven

Approval or Counter Offer

Occasionally, you will get a call from the loss mitigator but usually, you have to call them regularly to stay on top of what's happening with your deal. Almost always, when they do call you, it's because you are getting very near to at least verbal approval. Sometimes they will ask for updated financials and sometimes they want something ridiculous like a **missed initial** on the LISTING contract. (This actually happened to me!)

The ironic situation with the lenders is that they will spend 1 or 2 or 3 months looking at the offer and then will tell you that you have 24-48 hours to get them updated financials from your sellers that now live 1,000 miles away or else they will "close the file". Don't panic. You may not be able to do this but the fact that they even asked you usually means they are very close to approval. Call them or e-mail or fax them that you are working on it and will get it done ASAP. Sometimes the lender will go ahead and close the file anyway, but when you **do** get the paperwork in, they go ahead and open it back up and pick up where they left off. Even though they try to make it sound ominous and permanent, usually (there are some exceptions) it is no different than you *opening a file* folder to discuss the shortsale with the L.M. and then *closing the file* folder when you are done talking to them. Sometimes the L.M. just needs to make way for new files coming in and by "closing the file" it just gets opened by a new loss mitigator when you get the asked for stuff sent back in.

Unlike the President of the United States, the loss mitigator has the power of a "line item veto" when it comes to the HUD submitted with the shortsale package. The L.M. will call you up and say that they want to go over "some things" in the HUD that they need to clear up before you submit a new HUD that they will approve.

Everything is negotiations with the shortsale. Some of the LM's are even called loss negotiators. Even if you have someone do the negotiating for you from your side, it would be a great learning experience for you to do a few yourself. I personally will not give my negotiation business (shortsales and Loan Mods) to a total stranger or company but see nothing wrong with having a part time to full time assistant to handle all the lender calls and to call or e-mail owners, sellers, and buyers (or buyers agents) updates on status. You MUST however, learn negotiating yourself and train your assistant to the point that they are as good (or better) and experienced as you are (or will be) at it.

The first thing to learn about negotiating is to ask for more than you'll settle for and to ask for things you don't really care if you don't get them. Let me expand on that. If you would be happy with 6% commission, ask for 7% on the hud. If the buyers aren't asking for any seller concessions, ask for 5% in seller concessions. Ask for a $250 compliance fee, ask for a $200 property maintenance fee, ask for a $795 shortsale negotiating fee, if there is a second lien holder ask that they receive 20% of the lien, all to be paid by the lender. You will be surprised. I have actually gotten all of these things that the lender has paid for. They weren't all on the same deal, but the good thing is that I got any of them at all. It was just extra money that I wasn't counting on.

So you might ask if asking for all these things will kill the deal. Of course not. These are negotiating tools. The LM will go through the HUD with you and say well we can't allow this and we won't pay for that and this fee has to be lower, etc. and then ask you to submit a new HUD. If you got any of the stuff you asked for, great! If you didn't get any of the things mentioned, here is what you say when the lender wants the buyer to come up in price or for you to cut your commission or both... "the buyer is at their limit with the cash needed to come up with and what the monthly payment will be...they said this is as high as they can go...how about if I talk to the buyers and resubmit a new HUD with all the other stuff removed as you requested except for_____ and we can see if this comes close enough to your bottom line on this property?"

Of course, when you submit your hud to the 2nd lien holder (if any) you will show a token $1,000 going to them as the payoff. They will laugh or say "No way" and then tell you some figure they have in mind to accept. The amount they tell you they *absolutely* "Have to have" is **not**. They **will** take less. The figure they quote you is what they **hope** to get (just like you would **hope** to get 7 or 8% commission.) If they have already sold the loan to a collections company, it can get sticky since collection companies generally **expect** the property to get foreclosed, receive nothing, and then file a deficiency judgement to collect as much as they can.

Plain and simple, some loss negotiators will lie to you about what they are willing to pay and what their bottom line is. I've had them lie to me about how much the BPO came back at, (10k MORE than what a friend of mine that did the BPO told me was submitted) and then telling me they had to have the amount of the BPO. (Which wasn't true either) Hopefully, this book will keep you from asking for nothing and getting it. It would be great if you also learn enough so that the LM can't tell you are relatively new to shortsales. (less than 10 successfully closed) They will still try to bamboozle you, but with the info you have now you will see that this is all just negotiating and they are trained to say the things they do to **mitigate losses**. (loss mitigator...get it?) Keep in mind that many of them are new to the business also. I've talked to a couple of Flunkies that said stuff so stupid I asked if they were new and got, "How could you tell for a reply."

After everything is settled down the LM will either give you a verbal approval or say it's submitted for approved and it just needs to go to the investor on the loan for final approval. The loan is NOT approved until you receive **written** confirmation with a bottom line figure. It's been my experience that if an investor sees that the owner owns, and is living in a different house than the one being shortsold, and the home the owner owns and lives in is **not** in default of the loan, the investor typically asks the seller to sign an unsecured note for $25-35k at 0% interest for 10 years. If an investor sees the seller has $5ooo or more in the bank, the seller is often told to bring $2-3000 to the table or its no deal.

I've had sellers willing to comply with these requests and the deal has gone through and closed, and, I've had sellers refuse to cooperate and just let the home go to foreclosure. It's a tough sell since the homeowner is told from the beginning that a shortsale is the way to go since it doesn't cost them a dime out of their pocket and they can live in the house rent free while the sale process is going on. Lately, I've shied away from homeowners that don't live in the home being foreclosed. Like a shortsale with Countrywide, it is just not cost effective. I average between $100 and $300 per hour (depending on price) for time I spend on a typical shortsale. When Countrywide dipped below $10 per hour for the time spent, I quit doing them as shortsale or loan modification. I WILL do Countrywide IF the homeowner is someone I know, a referral, or a member of my church. I will do a second home if the homeowner is in default on all the property he owns. Otherwise, it just isn't worth the time. Remember in the first chapter I explained that you have to figure out how much you want to make each year, break it down into an hourly wage, and then see what you can eliminate or delegate if the activity doesn't get you your hourly rate.

Getting approval from the 2nd lien holder has become increasingly difficult as the number of shortsales has increased. In the old days, the 2nd lien holder would be glad to go quietly away for a measly 1000 bux. Nowadays, they are asking for as much as 80% of the 2nd lien amount. The current average received is right around 8.5% so don't let the 2nd mortgage people bully you or tell you some baloney about they are insured for 20% or that they want to see the house foreclosed if they don't get their money so they can sue. How ridiculous. Unfortunately, the 2nd DO try to hold the deal hostage sometimes. It depends how badly the first lender wants to get rid of the house without foreclosure costs and what they think the Realtor and buyer is willing to give up to make the deal go through. We are in a tough spot because on the one hand we want to see the deal go through and get paid for all our efforts. On the other hand, if we throw in the towel, we receive absolutely nothing (which is worse than little or no commission) AND the homeowner we've promised to help avoid foreclosure will get foreclosed. How would you feel if the homeowner KNEW the reason the deal fell through and the house foreclosed was that you wouldn't cut your commission? It would be a tough call for me and fortunately, I only cut it below 5% once and that was my second shortsale deal. I was desperate for the money and the home price was pretty high so that I still made more than I would have with an average price home at the typical local commission rate.

There have been some changes recently from some lenders (notably Countrywide-Bank of America) that reject ANY changes in the contract at all. The minimum 90 day approval process from Countrywide is worse now that the approval process has to start over at the very beginning if ANYTHING at all is changed on the contract – even if it is identical in every way except for a buyer name change. I've had buyers drop out (in the third month of negotiations) and had a backup contract for the exact same price and conditions which they started over from the very beginning. I don't know if it's libel or not so I **won't** say the people setting the policy for Countrywide-Bank of America are idiots. Admittedly, they sometimes consider special circumstances and occasionally let the process continue where it left off.

When it comes to the time for acceptance and the time for the closing dates on the purchase offer, it can vary wildly between lenders. The easiest way to handle this is to put in any agreeable date and note under the special clauses that buyer and seller agree to extend the offer for acceptance until 3rd party written approval and to extend closing date till 30-45 days after third party written acceptance. Note that buyer may rescind the offer at anytime prior to 3rd party written approval. (Remember, I'm not a Lawyer and contract Law is WAY out of my field.) You should also include under special clauses that the buyer may walk away at their option if the property is vandalized more than $500* in damages between purchase offer and closing. (*insert any figure the buyer is comfortable with)

You can choose anyway you like to handle multiple offers and there are some that disagree with me but here is the way I've found to be most fair to all:

The first person to put an offer in, that offer and ONLY that offer is submitted. Banks are easily confused with multiple offers and they function best when looking at only **one** offer at a time. (Be sure to *notify the seller of each offer as required by law.)* This can be verbal. IF the buyers hang in there, the bank either approves that offer or gives a counter offer (just like a normal sale) The first buyer then has the right to come up to meet the banks counter offer. (First right of refusal) If the buyers choose NOT to come up to the Banks counter offer, the next buyer offer in line is asked if THEY are willing to meet the bank counter offer. This continues if no buyer is willing until all buyers have been given the opportunity to match the banks counter offer. If no one is, the first person is asked to make their highest and best counter offer to the banks counteroffer. If they do not wish to counter, it goes down the line again. The next buyer in line is free to make a counter to the banks counter.

I'm often asked if the seller should sign a purchase offer before it is submitted to the lender. This is another area that some Realtors disagree with me. I do NOT have the seller sign the purchase offer. If the purchase offer is signed, by our MLS rules, the property must be listed as a pending contract. If the property is pended, you aren't too likely to get a back up offer.

When a property is headed for foreclosure, time is extremely important. The last thing you need is someone tying up the property for a month or two with a lowball offer and then have the lender say **no** a week before foreclosure or just as bad have the buyers walk just prior to 3rd party acceptance and you not having a back-up. Getting a better offer than the lowball in that short a time frame will be very difficult. Some lenders don't even ask for the sellers to sign the purchase offer until they are ready to approve it. The lender for the buyers will require a fully executed contract (as will the Title company before the loan can be processed and the sale closed. If the lender tells me they want the seller signature they are usually pretty close to approval and I don't mind taking it off the market and pending it. (and collecting the buyers deposit at that time) Don't pend properties without a deposit and don't take a deposit unless you're going to pend the property. If you insist on a deposit you are obligated to pend the property as well. If the LM asks for the purchase offer to be signed before they even begin the review (which happens sometimes) I go ahead, get the seller to sign, get the deposit, and pend the property.

In the LISTING that I ask the seller to sign, I put in two handwritten clauses:

1. Seller agrees to **any** price changes deemed necessary by the realtor-agent to get a good offer on this property.

2. Seller agrees to sign **any** purchase offer that the lender 3rd party approves of.

This saves a lot of time running back and forth to the seller for every price change and usually calms the lender about the seller not signing any old offer (or subsequent offers)that come in and wasting time. Often, investors will put in a real low offer and will not come up one dime over the original price they offered. If the property is taken off the market, (pended) this can kill a good offer from coming in. Once I have an offer on the property, I put in the MLS for any potential buyers agents to call me so that I can explain the situation to them and they can decide if they still want to go ahead and show the property knowing that any offer would be a backup. If the first offer IS from an investor with a real low offer, it is almost a sure bet that the bank will counter anyway. It also gives me the opportunity to tell them how far along we are in the process. Sometimes we are very near a decision from the lender and if the offer is close to getting approved they sometimes are willing to wait it out for a week or two and sometimes they just get lucky.

I had one deal that was incredible timing. At 10:00 A.M. a buyers agent called me and told me that his buyers were fed up with waiting for an answer and over the weekend, they put another offer in on another house and were withdrawing the offer on my house. A different agent called me about an hour later and asked me about the house and I told him there was currently NO offer and the lender was VERY close to making a decision. He showed the house about noon. The agent called me about one P.M. and said he was faxing over an offer. I got the offer about 1:30 and it was identical to the previously withdrawn offer. At 2 P.M. the LM for the lender called me and said the offer was being approved except for the junk fees I asked for. I told him the story of what had happened and he said, "Just get the new offer signed from the borrowers (that's what the lender calls your seller) and submit it with the new HUD and we'll get your approval letter sent to you before the end of the week.

I love a happy ending.

Chapter Eight

Things Happen

If you're at least 5 years old, you probably already know that things happen. Unplanned things. Things we wish hadn't happened. You also know that life isn't fair. If you're less than 20 you might still shout out, "But that isn't fair!" If you're older than 20 and still shouting out that isn't fair, you need a reality check. Mature up and take some responsibility. When unplanned things happen, (and they will) be resilient enough, persistent enough, resourceful enough, and smart enough. Think creatively on how to beat a particular obstacle to your successful closing. Talk to someone you know in the real estate field that has done many shortsales or has been in the business for many years. Ask them how they would solve the problem.

Believe it or not, sometimes the answer is in the challenging opportunity. (problem) I've had sellers that not only hadn't made their house payment for 8-10 months but they also had worked under the table and not filed an income tax form in 5 years. As you know by now, The financial statement, a copy of the last year or two taxes, and recent paystubs are normal requirements before a lender will consider a shortsale. This was one of my first deals and I had the flunkie ask her supervisor and a real loss mitigator if anything could be done to work this out. They suggested mentioning these things in the hardship letter, an additional separate page explaining the lack of tax forms, and an additional separate page explaining the lack of pay stubs. For good measure, I also had the reason, like, TAX FORMS and PAY STUBS in large letters at the top of the explanation page. That way the LM didn't just glance through and **not** see the tax forms or pay stubs and just bury it at the bottom of the pile as just another submission where the Realtor doesn't know how to properly submit a shortsale package. Working with as many files as they are, LM's do not waste their time on incomplete files or those that look like an incompetent sent them.

Sometimes the seller comes into sudden money from some source and is able to pay up the loan. Share their joy, withdraw the listing at no charge, shake their hand congratulating them, pick up your sign, and stay in touch. They will either know someone and refer them to you or they will be in dire straits **again** and remember how polite, kind, and gracious you were.

A few times, I've been working with sellers that felt they had no other option but to shortsale the property. The lender then has stepped in and offered a loan modification that was too good to refuse. Only a jerk would insist that they had agreed to sell the house and by golly you had worked hard on the shortsale and put a lot of time into it and they owed you for your time and trouble. Use the same pattern as the suddenly coming into money reaction. You are a professional and a mature professional doesn't whine, "it isn't fair!"

At the listing interview, I always question the sellers about the consideration of bankruptcy. If the house is the **only** reason they are considering bankruptcy, they should not consider it and I believe any competent bankruptcy attorney will tell them that. If they owe the IRS or a student loan or property taxes then a bankruptcy won't help them in that situation either. The problem with bankruptcy and shortsale is a lender cannot do a shortsale while the bankruptcy is in progress. A bankruptcy prohibits collection activity and a shortsale is considered collection activity. If the homeowner has filed or is planning to file for bankruptcy protection, you will not be able to shortsale the house.

Sometimes the homeowner will decide to wait until the house is shortsold before filing for bankruptcy. Some use the time of no mortgage payments to save up to pay the attorney. Some use the mortgage payments to pay down or off their other bills so that no bankruptcy is needed. When a lender has requested the seller to sign an unsecured note for multiple thousands of dollars, I've had the sellers agree and sign the note at closing and then file for bankruptcy the following week and include the note in the "to be discharged" debt.

The market changes. The market is different in different areas of the country and you should be in tune with what is happening in *your* area to keep on top of when changes occur and what types of changes are happening. Doing the BPO's for your properties to give to the BPO person should be a great help and working with buyers will also give you a feel for what's happening. Study your MLS statistics – How many house are on the market? How many are sold each month? What is the average price? Compare the stats for the last 3 months of this year with the same time period of last year. What is happening in your niche market? Currently in central Florida, for example, if your niche is condos you may need to get a day job and maybe a night job to supplement your income.

Buyers circumstances change. In the market I'm in, it has happened a few times that the potential buyer with a good job and steady employment has found themselves out of a job and little prospect of being able to replace their previous income. The economy is scaring a lot of would be buyers into more caution. Homes that were fantastic deals last year that sold as shortsales are currently upside down. Buyers are fearful that if the market continues to drop, it will be many years before they have even a little equity in their home. On the other hand, a person can own a great home for less than the equivalent to rent.

In that respect, it's hard to understand this:
A person buys a $300,000 home in 2006 with payments of $2500 per month PITI. The home is now worth $150,000. It can be rented for $1200 per month. Rather than shortsell the home, rent for 2-3 years at $1200 per month and then buy their old home back or it's equivalent for 150-160k, they will do a loan mod., pay $1800 per month for the next 30 years and owe more than the house will be worth for the next 15 years.

Buyers get tired of waiting. Even if the Realtor they are working with knows how to do shortsales, that doesn't mean the listing agent for the house knows what they are doing. The problem comes up that the shortsale is successful or not almost always depending on the listing Realtor. Many Realtors either won't or truly hate showing shortsale houses because of the average dismal success rate. As soon as you can, under the Realtor to Realtor comments on your shortsale listings, put something along the lines of "Successful Shortsale record" or "85% shortsale closing record" or even "Bring your shortsale buyer with confidence, I'll get the job done." When I only had 2 successful shortsales under my belt, I started putting in, "Agent does short sales exclusively". You will eventually get to the point where the Realtors that work with buyers will not be fearful of bringing you an offer. Because of the bad market for regular homes here, I've had other Realtors call me to shortsale **their** home for them and have given a simple referral fee for the agent to turn their sellers that need a shortsale over to me to handle for them.

Some other things that *can and do* crop up to put a "hiccup" in the smooth road to success are the lenders expecting us to cut our commissions, vandalism that sometimes occurs to the property if the homeowner moves out early, vandalism by the homeowner if the homeowner is a jerk, insufficient paperwork or paperwork that must constantly be updated because the LM took too long to move the deal along, closing the file because you didn't get them a silly scrap of paper within 24 hours when they request it after "reviewing " their file for 2 months, mechanics liens on the property, the second lien holder being stupid, (Hmmm... should I take $3,000 cash now or $0 later?) or even worse, selling off the 2nd for pennies on the dollar, charging off the loan and then having to deal with a collection agency.

Every once in a while you will get a slam dunk. A slam dunk is when there is one lien holder (so no chance of 2nd making outrageous demands), the homeowner is unemployed (so no chance of loan mod) there are no other bills or liens (so no chance of bankruptcy) it isn't a divorce situation, the person keeps a relatively neat home, no repairs are needed, the home is easy to show, the lender isn't Countrywide or Bank of America, the seller has an e-mail address and a fax machine, (or easy access) the lender is owed about what the home is worth, (or a little less) your sign brings in a lot of buyer calls, the home is within a couple of miles of your office, the lender doesn't cut your commission because it's also your buyer, you bring them an offer equivalent to the BPO, the seller was planning on moving out the week before closing is scheduled anyway, seller leaves the home clean and empty of all debris, seller leaves the appliances they said they would leave, the new lender appraises out, the home inspection and termite reveal no surprises, buyer is happy when they do the walk through, the closing goes smoothly, and you get a nice, big, commission check for all your hard (ha-ha) work.

Trust me, it is very rare but it **does** happen.

There is one **other** thing that is great about shortsales.

Because there are so many things that *can* go wrong and almost always do ...

Because it takes so much extra work and it always does ...

There is almost NO competition for anyone to do the shortsale market.

"Old" pros are used to the relative ease of the regular sales and find the shortsales distasteful. (*Relative* ease because most "regular" sales **also** have a tremendous load of problems) and there are some Realtors with many years of experience that have only done 0-2 shortsales in a 20+ year career.

"New" pros because they usually have enough problems just learning the basic "ins and outs" of regular real estate than to take the necessary time to learn a totally different aspect that even some experienced agents and relatively few brokers even know.

So, there is virtually no real competition if you should choose to become THE EXPERT at your local board.

Chapter Nine

Miscellaneous Stuff

If your broker has been a broker for a number of years, chances are that they no little or nothing about doing a successful shortsale in today's market. I don't mean that in a bad way, it's just that many brokers do not compete with their agents and if all they did was a couple of shortsales five or ten years ago, it's a whole new ballgame now. If they are taking 20-50% of your commission and are not helping you get the shortsale listing or helping you close the shortsale deal, you might consider switching brokers or renegotiating the commission split.

There are some good brokers out there and you must evaluate what the broker is offering to you compared to what you are getting in return. Do they give you leads? Does someone on "floor duty" get your sign calls? Does the broker take your sign calls? Does the broker pay for ads? Are they working? Are you supplied with a desk space that you don't use because you work out of your home? Does the broker have a good reputation with cooperating agents and brokers? Does the broker "force" you to use their closing agent, their mortgage company, their buyers warranty? Their home inspection company? Are you free to legally market the home as you see fit? Are you forced to answer the phones for the company on "floor time?" Are you expected to do "company things" which take away from your time?

120

In the end, all that we have is time. There is work time and there is family time, and friends time. (and God time which is better addressed in other books) It is somewhat of a balancing act. Time at work takes time away from family. Time with family takes time away from work. Real estate has been known to be an all consuming career littered with workaholics that succeed financially as their family life crumbles. There are also the lazy that got into real estate believing the late nite "gurus" about making a million dollars a year almost effortlessly. They don't last long because hardly any deals just "fall in your lap like the gurus would have you believe.

When you set your goals, make sure they cover all areas of your life and are reasonably balanced. Personally, I would rather have my kid saying, "My Dad came to every one of my games, cheered me on, and was proud of me whether we won or lost. He never considered it time wasted." Instead of, "My Dad was hardly ever around and I barely knew him growing up, but he always bought me whatever I wanted."

When you get older and have the time to reflect, what will you wish you had done differently? Will you think to yourself, "if only I had worked an hour more hour each day and a few hours extra on Saturday." Or will it be, "if only I had spent an hour more each day with my family and got together for food, fun and fellowship each Saturday." Don't say either! I want you to eliminate three phrases entirely from your vocabulary. By doing this, you will grow up, live a better life, and be happier.

1. If only...

2. But ...

3. I wish ...

These are the beginning words of excuses which should have absolutely no place in your vocabulary. If someone else **has** done it, **then you can do it.** If someone else **has never** done it, then **you can be the first.**

Make a schedule and adhere to it. One of the most successful Realtors decided how much money he wanted to make so he broke it down from year to month to week to day to hour. Then he asked himself, "If I had an employee and I agreed to pay this amount of money, what would I expect from my employee to earn this amount of money from me?" Do you think you'd like them to come in early? Stay late? Work Saturdays? Work off the clock? Learn and study on their own time to become an expert in your field? ... Answer these questions and you'll have some idea of what it's going to take to reach your goals.

When it comes to marketing, I spend a minimal amount for a reason. I list the property and rarely work with buyers. My marketing is the price of the property which I can change at will. My marketing is to other Realtors who work with buyers that want a good deal. Always be polite and fair and gracious to other Realtors. If they get crossed by you, they will NOT show your houses or bring you offers. Even though you'll have enough deals going on in a few months that 1 or 2 falling through won't faze you, remember that the other Realtor only averages 3-4 closed sides per year and something falling through (which will happen sometimes, nobody has a perfect record) can be devastating to them. Some of them will only make up their marketing costs if the sale goes through.

An unbelievable amount of dollars is spent on advertising or marketing. Billboards, benches, grocery receipts, "farm" newsletters, open houses, Realtor magazines, classified ads. There are all kinds of marketing gimmicks and Realtors on average spend a lot of money to get that buyer to call. Since other Realtors are spending all that money to grab those buyers, why should you or I? There are only so many buyers out there that are ready, willing and able to buy a home. If less than 200 homes are bought each month in your county or working area, do you think spending an extra $10,000 per month would increase the number that are going to buy? How about $100,000? Yes, more would buy from YOU... MAYBE. If all your listed homes are **below market value,** do you think you'll have any trouble getting an offer from another Realtor?

If you have absolutely NO assistance and are completely on your own, how many ready, willing, and able **buyers** can you work with at any given time and give good service to? 5? 8? I submit to you that more than 10 is physically impossible and the marketing costs to capture that many qualified buyers would be prohibitive.

NOW...How many listings or **sellers** can you handle and give good service to at any given time? 20? 25? I submit to you that up to 30 is still within reason. Working alone, with no assistance. Short sales, doing all the calling and negotiating yourself. Don't even get me started on how many **regular** listings you can handle. At least 30, maybe 40 and up to 50... by yourself alone. So here's a tip... have at least 3 times as many sides close with 1/3 the marketing cost by concentrating on being a listing agent.

What about training? There are a whole slew of trainers, mentors, and "gurus" out there that want to take your money. There are $2500 and up weekend "bootcamps," there are $99 per month "universities" (12 month minimum sign up) and there are all kinds of books and cd's and dvd's that will reveal "secrets" that some guy just "stumbled upon." Even though the guy that stumbled on these secrets, tricks, or techniques is sposed to be making $4,000 a DAY with these techniques, he is willing to share them with you for a paltry sum of $149, $379 or $1799 ... depending on which "secrets" or program or system you buy into. Why do these "gurus" want to share their secrets with you for such a pittance? They say they want to "give back" ... to help other poor, struggling slobs like they were to be rich and happy and successful like they now portray themselves to be.

I want to save you time and money by revealing two secrets MY mentor (Zig Ziglar) told me. He didn't even charge me for this knowledge as I am not going to charge you. (other than you bought this book to learn more about shortsales and I have nothing else to sell to you.)

The first secret is ... there are NO secrets. If the guru that "stumbled upon" his system or plan or "trick, scheme or device" has told *anyone* else about it, then it is no longer a secret. If no one else previously knew about the "secret" method devised, then the information is really just a melding of a few different old ideas into a new one. The truth is, some of these "secrets" are either immoral or illegal. When a "guru" advises you to use any of these secrets, he generally hasn't done them himself, and you could go broke, (or to be politically correct, have a *negative net worth*) or what they advise you to do is illegal in your state. If you try one of his "techniques" and get sued or arrested, is the guru going to have his army of lawyers swoop down and rescue you?

One of the "gurus' that revealed all kinds of "secrets" is still doing jail time here in Florida ... and I still have his "course" I bought 15 years ago for $39.00 cash! Oh yeah! One other method the "guru's have of "hooking" you is to offer you something for free or at a nominal cost like $1.00 or $7.95 shipping and they give you a little bit of information. The "real secrets" will be revealed shortly in the months to come with their monthly newsletters and webinars. The cost is "free" ... for the first thirty days. If you don't go through the arduous process of getting **out** of "the club" or the "group" or the "inner Circle" or "insiders," then your credit card will be charged $79.- $199 per MONTH. Sadly, most people forget to get out and will lose at *least* one months worth which you will have a REALLY hard time getting back or even getting the withdrawals stopped. The "guru's" make their money on people that don't realize the "bonus" for buying their stuff is "free" 30 day membership. Go ahead and see what happens if you ask for just the book or cd at the nominal charge and ask that the "Bonus" membership NOT be included. They won't agree to "give you" anything without including the bonus. They've never explained to me how a "**bonus**" can be a **requirement** of an offer. The **bonus** in this case is actually a **condition** of the offer, not a **real** bonus. I know you've **never** worked for a place where they told you that one of their conditions and requirements of employment is that you MUST accept a bonus with the job.

The second secret isn't really a secret at all. It's written in the Bible. The second "secret" is:

"The learning is in the doing."

The word **disciple** means "one who learns by doing." Think about it. Everything you have **truly** learned, you've learned by doing. There are books on the martial arts. How do you think a person would fare if they had read **every** martial arts book there was and then fought against an opponent that hadn't read a single book but had sparred and practiced for just one full week? When Doctors go to medical school do you think they just read about surgery and medicine, graduate and open up a practice? Or do they spend years working at the hospital with an internship as they practice their practice? Teachers don't really learn how to teach until they start teaching. Lawyers don't HAVE a practice unless they practice. Trucking school (to drive the 18 wheelers) has very little bookwork and many, many hours of actually driving and maneuvering before they are deemed qualified to drive *without* a trainer. Doing IS the ultimate in learning.

So even more important than this book is actually **getting out of the office** and meeting face to face with as many potential listers as you can. Force yourself to go talk to people. It's scary at first, but besides the learning being in the doing, the more you do something (practice) the better you'll get at it. The better you get at something, the more you'll enjoy it. The more you enjoy something, the more you'll want to do it. Except for spending time with my wife there are few things I enjoy more than getting in my car with a list of recent default notices and driving out to talk to these potential listers in person. Letting them tell you their story and then actually being able to help them out of the sad situation many of them are in is a good feeling. It is also great to have them invite you in and then list their house with you on the spot.

Don't be an "average' agent. The average agent in the U.S. does a total of 3 sides per year. They get listings and sales almost totally from friends, family, church or other group affiliations, and "floor time" sitting in the office. Don't think for a moment that a top producer does that. If you don't have a top producer in your office that will allow you to "model" or "mimic what they are doing and how they are doing it, just watch the average person in your office that **isn't** doing that well and then **do the opposite.**

DON'T sit around the office shuffling paperwork from one side of the desk to another. Don't spend more than necessary time talking with other agents – they will never buy a house from you or give you a referral. Talking to people you know is easy. Agents that only talk to people they are business associated with will not succeed. You MUST talk with total strangers regularly and often. You will be amazed at how desperate some people will be to talk to another rational adult. Fortunately, if the other person simply wants to gab, gossip, and gripe, you have an appointment you must leave for immediately. (wink, wink) Keep going, you'll find someone that wants to talk business.

I like numbers. Numbers can tell you where you are, where you have been, and more importantly, what you will have to do to hit the numbers you set for your goal. Things may be different in your area, but what I have found by actually going to the door are my numbers. Keep track of your own numbers so you won't get discouraged. I have found that when I go to a house that has been served a Notice of Default or Lis Pendens, that between 20-25% have already moved out. I used to try to track them down and tried paying for a locating service but timewise and moneywise, it just wasn't worth it. For every person that actually speaks with me face to face, one out of four ends up listing with me. About one out of thirty face to face meetings ends up with me listing the house right there on the spot at the first visit. Why are these numbers important? Because I've had it happen that I've seen 15 people face to face in a row and not gotten a single listing. That's discouraging. I've also had it happen that 3 face to face visits in a row have resulted in 3 listings. Don't let temporary appearances sway you from your goals. I've had times where I've spent the entire day trying to see people and not seen a single one. I've also had days where I've seen people and gotten 3 listings in a single day. Sales are a numbers game and **everything works out if you do the work.**

My sales mentor, started out selling pots and pans door to door. He figured his numbers and realized that he could reach his goals by asking 8 women a week to have a "party" in their home where he would cook the meal and supply the food for all invited. He broke it down further and realized that he made $11 (This was 40 years ago when $11 was like twice a "good" hourly wage) every time he knocked on a door. No matter what. If no one was home, if they said "no", if they cursed him and slammed the door in his face … the **numbers** said it was worth $11 dollars to him. He said he would literally skip for joy when no one was home because that was a very fast $11 to him in the big picture. Try it yourself. (after a year of keeping track) Do you think I don't enjoy going knocking on "default doors" when I know it's worth $94 dollars to me for **every** door I knock on? **No matter** if it's vacant, if no one's home, or I get the door slammed in my face. (some people are in strong denial) EVERY door is worth $94 to me. Is that a good hourly wage? Did you figure out that going to just 2 default doors **a day** would get you more than the income of the average real estate BROKER in America?

While you are learning by doing, you also need to spend some time "book larnin" time also. There are numerous free you tube videos and websites where one can learn a ton of stuff absolutely free of charge. Every one that offers you free stuff will want you to buy some other stuff. You give up your e-mail and they send you a free mini-course which will allude to bigger and better secrets in their 'pay for" course. Some is inexpensive and some is outrageous. Some is re-packaged old information and some is just plain wrong. Heck, I'm only telling you what I believe is true right now. I'm not telling you I'm right about everything I say or that I won't change my mind. I DO know that the market is always changing and the laws are always changing and the way people do business is always changing. I like the Shortsale Daily News, Pre-foreclosure Daily Grind and Friday coffee break with Pat Precourt, all on the internet. They give great information for free and they are also Realtors. Harris Real Estate University also gives out a ton of good, free information by way of webinars which you can download onto a disc and listen to while you're driving.

There are plenty of "offers" on the internet concerning shortsales and if you should choose to purchase any, that's entirely up to you. It's kind of like Radio. If you want to listen to informative talk shows, there will be a load of commercials. Some of the commercials will be to sell you a load of baloney. Some will be good stuff. I have bought numerous $20-40 dollar books and

I've paid for the full year at Harris Real Estate University. I guess it depends on how much is a lot of money to you and how much you're willing to spend. Online **Free** is always my favorite option because it's so easy to get all your money back.

If you're a 20 year vet, you already know the final advice I'm going to give. If you're a relative newcomer, you'll learn soon enough. Just like every other profession, you will encounter what I scientifically call "weirdos". Not everyone in each group and actually a very small percentage actually **are** weirdos. These are the ones that make the game of Real Estate so interesting. There are weird buyers. There are weird sellers. There are weird agents. There are weird Brokers. There are weird mortgage brokers. There are weird lenders and there are some weird people involved in all stages of every real estate transaction. Rejoice in them. They make the deal interesting and later on you'll have fond memories to laugh about when you reflect on your Real Estate career. After a while, you will barely remember the totally sane people you've worked with. You **will** remember the really weird people.

APPENDIX   A

Documents for a complete shortsale package

1.) **Letter of Authorization** - Make sure this is sent separately as soon as you take the listing to make sure you have all the right numbers to call and fax to and to find out if the loan has been sold. The Authorization letter is usually sent to a different fax number than the shortsale package so be sure to get the correct number for which item you are sending.

2.) **Hud -1** (This is the bank's bottom line statement.) Make sure you ask for ½ to 1% more for commission and $200 to $300 compliance fee and the other "junk" fees mentioned earlier. You probably won't get them but it never hurts to ask.

3.) **Purchase offer** – Make sure the buyer has signed it and depending on how you want to do it – your seller. Make sure to ask for 5% concession in buyers closing costs from the seller(Lender)

4.) **Hardship letter** (signed and dated)

5.) **Supporting hardship information** if any (letter of Termination, Medical Bills, repair bills, etc.)

6.) **Copies of 2 most recent months (60 to 90 days old at most) bank statements.** If seller no longer has a bank account, get a letter signed and dated that they no longer have an account. If possible, show the closeout statement. (For example, account is **overdrawn** $43.83)

7.) **Copies of 2 most recent paystubs**. (must not be more than 60 days old) If seller is collecting unemployment, there will be no proof except for the deposits to the bank account. Circle the deposits from unemployment on the bank statement and notate it that this irs the only record of the unemployment compensation. If unemployed and no compensation, have the seller sign and date a statement to that effect.

8.) **Last 2 years tax returns including the w-2's**. Usually only the top 3 pages are needed and depending on the time of year (Like the first 3 months and last 2 months of the year) only one year is necessary. If self employed, they sometimes want to see the entire return. If the seller owns a business, the lender likes to see a profit and loss statement going back to when the first payment or 2 was missed.

9.) **Divorce decree if applicable**. If a couple was married at the time of the house purchase or if they were married after the time of the house purchase, the lender will want to see the divorce decree to see how the judge dispensed the property and how much there was.

10.) **Bankruptcy discharge if applicable.** If the bankruptcy has already been discharged, the lender may proceed with the foreclosure petition. If sellers filed for bankruptcy and it has not yet been discharged, the lender cannot due a shortsale since a shortsale is considered a collection activity and prohibited by bankruptcy laws. The seller should be encouraged to wait to file for bankruptcy until after the shortsale is completed.

11.) **Signed listing agreement and copy of the actual MLS listing**. Lately the lenders have been asking to see the actual listing itself since being on the MLS is a requirement but anybody can fill out a worthless listing form.

12.) **Comparables** (make sure they are low) with **listing history.** The listing history simply shows the lender that you made the effort to sell the property for more. I also show them at which point we start getting numerous calls from agents and buyers expressing an interest in the property. For example:

Starting price: (current market value or slightly below)
$180,000 on 01/10/09   price drop to:
$175,000 on 01/25/09   price drop to:
$170,000 on 02/10/09   price drop to:
$165,000 on 02/25/09 (some interest shown)   price drop to:
$160,000 on 03/10/09 (a lot of interest shown)   price drop to:
$155,000 on 03/25/09 Purchase offer comes in at $150,000

13.) Make sure to take **photos of any defects** in the property and to write a short page **listing all the defects** because the BPO person won't always use your stuff and the bPO person will never look into how many vacant houses or sexual predators are in the area.

When taking the listing, always ask for the last payment statement from the Lender. This insures the correct loan number and the correct loan servicer at the recent time. This is **not** to be included in the shortsale package but it is helpful paperwork to have.

Be sure to write the loan number for the 1st and the second on **every** piece of paper. Be sure to specify which is the first lien loan number and which is the second lien loan number.

Appendix B   Sample Letter of Authorization

Authorization To Release Information

Date: _____ This document is to be continuously valid until or unless rescinded by the owner/borrower.

1st Servicer Name _____ Loan # _____

2nd Servicer Name_____ Loan # _____

Property Address; _____

_____

I/We, _____ authorize you to release any and all information to Jeffrey Smith, xxxx xxxxx and/or xxxx xxxxxx that he/she may require regarding my loan on the above referenced property. You may reproduce this document to acquire reference from more than one source.

Jeffrey Smith	Assistant or' partner	Mary xxxxxxx or customer
Shortsale Specialist	Realtor – Generic Realty	care @First American Title
(352) xxx-xxxx	(352) xxx-xxxx	(877)-xxx-xxxx
Jeff.shortsal@gmail.com	xxxxxxxxx@gmail.com	xxxxxxxx@firstam.com
Fax: 866-xxx-xxxx	Fax: 866-xxx-xxxx	Fax: 866-xxx-xxxx

_____   _____
Borrower Printed Name   **Co-Borrower Printed Name**

_____   Last 4 digits of S.S. # _____
Borrower Signature

_____   Last 4 digits of S.S. # _____
Co-Borrower Signature

Feel free to use all the forms here and substitute names and phone numbers that are relevant to your personal use. The same goes for the Checklist form from appendix C. I usually leave this with the homeowner if they say they can't get all the papers they need while I am there. This checklist is a guide to help them remember. Get the authorization form signed while you are there getting the listing signed with the loan number. Then fax in the authorization form and the other papers don't **need** to be gathered until there is a written offer on the table. The checklist helps them keep in mind what they will need to do like save their paystubs and bank statements or get a copy of their tax returns, etc.

I didn't include a financial form because I couldn't break down a full 8.5 x 11 worksheet to reduce legibly to the 6x9 book format so when you send in the authorization for the first few, simply ask them to send you the financial worksheet that THEY use. You'll find they are all pretty much the same. I got my first financial form this way.

If you've read this far, congratulations! You now have my permission to e-mail me at the address given in the forms and ask me any 5 questions you may have concerning the shortsale.

Appendix   C   Short sale checklist

Short Sale Checklist

Property Address: _____

Borrower:_____

Servicer #1:_____Loan #:_____

Servicer #2:_____Loan #:_____

_____   Authorization to Release Information

_____   Client Financial Sheet (may be specific to lender)

_____   Hardship Letter (handwritten, signed and dated)

_____   Supporting Hardship Information (letter of termination,

       medical bills, repair bills, etc.)

_____   Copies of 2 most recent months checking account

_____   Copies of 2 most recent pay stubs

_____   Last year tax return with W-2's

_____   Divorce Decree (if applicable)

_____   Payment coupon from Lender

Jeffrey Smith	Snail mail Address:	e-mail address:
Xxxxxxxx Realty	123 Main St.	jeff.shortsale@gmail.com
Cell: xxx.xxx.xxxx	Central, Florida	
Fax: xxx.xxx.xxxx	12345-4321	

ABOUT THE AUTHOR

Jeffrey Smith is currently a licensed Realtor and a licensed Mortgage Broker.

Shortly after graduating from Florida State University, Jeff obtained his first real estate license in 1976 and began selling full time in the Orlando area. Many years passed and one of his moves was to Lake County in 2005. (About 30 miles NW of Orlando) When the economy changed dramatically at the last quarter of 2007, he saw the "writing on the wall" and began to deal strictly with homeowners that were about to lose their homes. He currently lives and works in Lake County, Florida. His incredible wife Gail has been an R.N. for almost 35 years and recently got her license also. They are looking forward to working together in real estate as they go into semi-retirement.

<u>Recommendations</u>

Free 52 lesson e-course (one per week) from the pre-foreclosure daily grind. (Bob LaChance)

The Short Sale Daily News – keep up with all the latest changes. Article format discusses changes which are happening regularly in the shortsale field. You can have your e-mail notified when a new shortsale article comes up. (This is free)

Friday Morning Coffee break – Pat Precourt answers questions honestly concerning shortsales in short 10 minute or less videos. You can send in questions of your own.(This is free)

Rapidfax – Don't waste money with a separate fax line and don't waste paper. Print out only the pages you need. This converts all incoming faxes (and gives you your own 800 type fax number) to a pdf file.

1.) I print out the pages I need for submission.

2.) Put the loan number on everything.

3.) Take 2 seconds to switch phone line to my fax machine.

4.) Fax necessary papers to **my** rapidfax 800 #.

5.) Fax everything just received to the lender with a click.

6.) Copy the pdf file and also e-mail it to the LM.

Everything is done in about 2 minutes total.

Total cost for everything including personal 800 #, faxes in, conversion to pdf, faxes out to **any** number (800 or not) and e-mail notification of incoming and outgoing successful fax is $9.95 per month. – a lot cheaper than a private fax line.

Made in the USA
Lexington, KY
13 October 2010